THE WAY
OF THE
WIZARD

Also by Deepak Chopra

Creating Health

Return of the Rishi

Quantum Healing

Perfect Health

Unconditional Life

Ageless Body, Timeless Mind

Journey into Healing

Creating Affluence

Perfect Weight

Restful Sleep

The Seven Spiritual Laws of Success

The Return of Merlin

Boundless Energy

Perfect Digestion

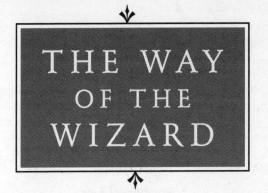

THE WAY
OF THE
WIZARD

Twenty
Spiritual Lessons
for Creating
the Life
You Want

DEEPAK CHOPRA

RIDER
LONDON · SYDNEY · AUCKLAND · JOHANNESBURG

3 5 7 9 10 8 6 4

First published by Harmony Books, a division of Crown Publishers, Inc., New York.

This edition published in 1996 by Rider,
an imprint of Ebury Press, Random House,
20 Vauxhall Bridge Road, London SW1V 2SA

Random House Australia (Pty) Limited,
20 Alfred Street, Milsons Point, Sydney,
New South Wales 2061, Australia

Random House New Zealand Limited,
18 Poland Road, Glenfield,
Auckland 10, New Zealand

Random House South Africa (Pty) Limited
PO Box 337, Bergvlei, South Africa

Random House UK Limited Reg. No. 954009

Papers used by Rider are natural, recyclable products made from wood grown in sustainable forests.

Printed in Great Britain by MacKays of Chatham

A CIP catalogue record for this book is available from the British Library

ISBN 0-7126-7207-9

Acknowledgments

I would like to express my love and gratitude to the following people:

First and foremost to my longtime friend, guide, and editor, Peter Guzzardi. Peter, you're the best!

And to my family at Harmony Books, including Shaye Areheart, Patty Eddy, Tina Constable, Leslie Meredith, Chip Gibson, and Michelle Sidrane.

Rita Chopra, Mallika Chopra, and Gautama Chopra for being the living expression of the principles in this book.

Ray Chambers, Gayle Rose, Adrianna Nienow, David Simon, George Harrison, Olivia Harrison, Naomi Judd, Demi Moore, and Alice Walton for their courage and commitment to a vision that is beyond all limitations.

Roger Gabriel, Brent Becvar, Rose Bueno-Murphy, and all my staff at the Sharp Center for Mind-Body Medicine for being inspiring examples to all our guests and patients.

Deepak Singh, Geeta Singh, and all my staff at Quantum Publications for their unflagging energy and dedication.

Muriel Nellis for her unflinching intention to maintain the highest level of integrity in all our endeavors.

Richard Perl for being such a great example of self-referral.

Arielle Ford for her unshakable faith in self-knowledge and her infectious enthusiasm and commitment to transform the lives of so many people.

And Bill Elkus for his understanding and friendship.

Part One
ENTERING THE WIZARD'S WORLD

People want to know why I, who come from India, am so interested in wizards. My answer is this: in India we still believe that wizards exist. What is a wizard? Not someone who can simply perform magic but someone who can cause transformation.

A wizard can turn fear to joy, frustration to fulfillment.

A wizard can turn the time-bound into the timeless.

A wizard can carry you beyond limitations into the boundless.

When I was growing up in India, I knew that all this was true. Sometimes old men in white robes and sandals came to our house, and even to a wide-eyed boy, they appeared to be very special creatures. They were completely at peace; they emanated joy and love; the wild ups and downs of everyday life seemed not to touch them at all. We called them gurus or spiritual counselors. But it took me a long time to realize that gurus and wizards are the same thing. Every society has had its teachers, seers, and healers; *guru* was just our word for those who had spiritual wisdom.

In the West a wizard is primarily thought to be a magician who practices alchemy, turning base metal into gold. Alchemy also exists in India (in fact it was invented there), but the word *alchemy* is really a code word. It stands for turning human beings into gold, turning our base qualities of fear, ignorance, hatred, and shame into the most precious stuff there is: love and fulfillment. So a teacher who can teach you how to turn yourself into a free, loving person is by definition an alchemist—and has always been one.

When I got to high school in New Delhi, I already knew a

lot about the most famous wizard in the Western tradition, Merlin. Like everyone, I loved him immediately. Soon the whole of his world opened up. In my head I still hold dozens of stanzas of Tennyson's epic poem *Idylls of the King,* which we were made to memorize on long, hot schooldays back then. I devoured every other source of Arthurian lore I could lay my hands on. It didn't seem unusual to me that I knew all about mild, green Camelot even though I lived under a fierce tropical sun, that I wanted to ride like Lancelot, even though I would have suffocated in armor, or that Merlin's crystal cave really existed, despite every author assuring me that wizards were mythical.

I knew differently, because I was an Indian boy, and I had met them.

WHY WE NEED WIZARDS

For thirty years I've thought about the wizard's knowledge. I've trekked to Glastonbury and the West Country, climbed the Tor, and seen the hill where Arthur and his knights are supposed to be sleeping. But something more mystical, the need for transformation, keeps pulling me back to wizardry. Each year I've felt that our times need this knowledge more than ever. Now that I've grown up, I spend my professional time talking and writing about how to achieve complete freedom and fulfillment. Only recently did I realize that what I'm talking about is alchemy.

Finally I decided that an exciting way to approach this topic would be through one of the most wondrous relationships ever recorded, that between Merlin and the boy Arthur in the crystal cave. As this book presents it, the crystal cave is a privileged place inside the human heart. It is the refuge of safety where a wise voice knows no fear, where the turmoil of the outside world cannot enter. In the crystal cave there has always been a wizard and always will be—you only have to enter and listen.

Modern people live in the wizard's world as much as past

generations did. Joseph Campbell, the great teacher of mythology, said that anyone standing on a street corner waiting for the light to turn green is waiting to step into the world of heroic deeds and mythic action. We just don't see our chance. We cross the street not noticing the sword in the stone standing by the curb.

The journey into the miraculous begins here. Now is the best time to start. The way of the wizard doesn't exist in time—it is everywhere and nowhere. It belongs to everyone and no one. So this is just a book about reclaiming what is already yours. As the first sentence of the first lesson says,

A wizard exists in all of us.
This wizard sees and knows everything.

This is the only sentence of the book you will have to take on trust. Once you find the wizard within, the teaching goes by itself. For many years this kind of spontaneous learning has been the center of my own daily life, watching and waiting for what the inner guide has to say. No other way of learning is so fascinating. I've heard Merlin speak from laughter overheard at the airport, from whispering trees on a walk down to the beach, even from my television. A bus station can turn into the crystal cave if you are open to it.

Why do we need the wizard's way? We need it to lift us from the ordinary and the humdrum to the kind of significance that we tend to relegate to myth but is actually right at hand, here and now. Being alive means winning the right to say anything you want, to be who you want to be, and to do what you want to do. Camelot was a symbol for this sort of freedom. That is why we look back upon Camelot with such wistfulness and admiration. Life has been difficult ever since.

A disciple once went to a great master and said, "Why do I feel so bottled up inside, as if I want to scream?" The master looked at him and replied, "Because everyone feels that way."

All of us want to expand in love and creativity, to explore our spiritual nature, yet often we fall short. We lock ourselves in our own prisons. Some people, however, have broken out of the confines that make life so constricted. Listen to the Persian poet Rumi, who says, "You are the unconditioned spirit trapped in conditions, like the sun in eclipse."

This is the voice of a wizard, who will not accept that humans are limited in time and space. We are just temporarily in eclipse. The purpose of learning from a wizard is finding the wizard within. Having found the inner guide, you've found yourself. The self is the ever-shining sun that may be in eclipse, but once the shadows pass, the sun is simply there in all its glory.

HOW TO LEARN FROM THE WIZARD

There are twenty lessons in this book, each told from the wizard's point of view. At the beginning of each lesson are some aphorisms, pithy bits of the wizard's wisdom to help you transcend ordinary reality. Read each one and let it sink in. Don't wait for a result, just allow yourself the experience. You don't have to work or apply effort. Effort is like struggling to get out of quicksand—it only pulls you in deeper.

The inner wizard wants to speak, and this is true for all of us. But the wizard needs a chance, an opening. Like Zen koans, aphorisms provide that opening by causing a shift in perception, which can trigger a shift in personal reality.

The wizard's voice needs to be brought back into daily life. I've quoted the first sentence of the first lesson: *A wizard exists in all of us. This wizard sees and knows everything.* The rest of the lesson goes as follows:

*The wizard is beyond opposites of light and dark,
good and evil, pleasure and pain.*

*Everything the wizard sees has its roots
in the unseen world.*

Nature reflects the moods of the wizard.

*The body and the mind may sleep,
but the wizard is always awake.*

The wizard possesses the secret of immortality.

If these words give you a faint tingle, a thrill of recognition, they have done their work. It is indeed thrilling to discover that you are not a constricted being but a child of the miraculous. That is the truth, the one deep fact about each of us that has been in eclipse far too long.

I've gathered together about a hundred such sayings, which are illustrated by stories from the world of Merlin and Arthur. These are not fragments from the old legends but parables I have set in that time. Sometimes the illustrative story doesn't seem to fit the aphorisms exactly or with perfect logic. That is deliberate, because the linear mind, with its need to create order, isn't the only part of yourself that is going to walk the wizard's way. You are going to walk it in imagination, in hope, in creativity, in love.

In short, the wizard's way is the way of spirit. But spirituality isn't opposed to rationality; it is the larger framework that reason fits into, one piece among many. To speak to the linear mind, I've provided a section called "Understanding the Lesson," which supports the aphorisms and the stories. Lastly comes "Living with the Lesson," in which I help you allow the wizard's wisdom to sink into your own experience.

"Living with the Lesson" is the active part of the wizard's way. My suggestions are simply a beginning, ways to spark your own participation. Ultimately it is your understanding that is going to change your reality. "Living with the Lesson" includes some exercises that may seem passive, because most of them are thought experiments.

What is a thought experiment? It's a way of leading your mind into new places, making it see things differently. The wizards knew something deep and important—if you want to change the world, change your attitude toward it. Einstein once lay on a couch, closed his eyes, and saw a man traveling at the speed of light. Following up on this intriguing image, he began to conduct various thought experiments, seemingly mere musings. Within a few years, however, the attitudes of the whole scientific world would be transformed as nature itself confirmed Einstein's transcendent visions.

If a fantasy on a couch can alter the world, then there must be tremendous power in thought experiments. Nothing is truly learned until it is lived. Reason, experience, spirit—once these come together, the wizard's way is open, the stage is set for alchemy. The wisdom inside you is like a spark that once lit can never be extinguished.

To put it all together, I suggest the following approach:

1. Sit quietly for a moment before you read any particular lesson.

2. Read the aphorisms and then sit for a few minutes to absorb them. Reread them as often as you like. Allow yourself an opportunity for your own reactions and insights—these are often the most valuable things you can receive.

3. Go on and read the rest of the material for that lesson: the Merlin and Arthur story, the section called "Understanding the Lesson," and the section called "Living with the Lesson."

4. If "Living with the Lesson" contains a practical exercise— most do—give yourself a few minutes to do the exercise. It is helpful to repeat it throughout the day if you want to get the full experience.

Reread each lesson as often as you want, one or more times; take a day or a week to live with it. There is no timetable for this process. I'd only caution that you should live with each lesson for at least one day rather than rush to absorb too many at a time.

THE SEVEN STEPS OF ALCHEMY

Part III of this book deals with the stages of transformation that the wizard takes his disciple through. I call these the seven steps of alchemy, which begin at birth and lead, eventually, to total transformation. Alchemy is about turning things to gold, that perfect, incorruptible substance. In human terms gold is a symbol for pure spirit. If a person gets beyond all limitation, throws off all fear, and realizes the pure spirit inside, then the seven steps of alchemy have been taken.

No journey is more wondrous. In Arthurian times they would have called it a quest, and the supreme object of such questing was always the Holy Grail, itself the most powerful symbol we have for pure spirit. So to me, alchemy and the Grail are the same thing. In both cases there is a deep search for the timeless aspect of life that brings what everyone dreams of—pure love, pure joy, pure fulfillment in spirit.

It doesn't matter whether you read Part II or Part III first. Each part has its own style and approach, but both come from the wizard's world. Merlin lives in both, and his purpose is always the same—to teach each of us how to attain the perfection that flesh should be heir to.

Finally, this book outlines a quest that will take you from a life dominated by the ego and all its struggle to a new life dominated by miracles. No two people learn at the same pace, but the hunger for miracles is so strong in everyone that I wish I could be with you the day that this wizard's knowledge really begins to dawn, and with it your new life. Nothing less than the full blossoming of your spiritual potential awaits you.

Note: Being a seer, the wizard has no gender, and it is only the clumsiness of English that turns Merlin into a "he" (as our language does with *God, prophet, seer,* and many other words that are far beyond male and female). *Wizardess* is a clumsy word, so please know that *wizard* applies to women as well as men. If anything, the return of the magical has been greeted more quickly by women in our society than by anyone else.

Part Two

THE WIZARD'S WAY

"There is a teaching," Merlin said, "called the way of the wizard. Have you heard of it?"

The boy Arthur looked up from building the fire, which wasn't going well. Building a fire rarely went well on the damp mornings of early spring in the West Country.

"No, I've never heard of that," Arthur said, after a moment's consideration. "Wizards? Do you mean they do things a different way?"

"No, just the way we do," Merlin replied. With a flick of his finger he lit the soggy heap of kindling that Arthur had gathered, having grown impatient with the boy's clumsy attempts at fire building. A blaze leapt up on the instant. Merlin then opened his hands and produced some food out of thin air—two russet potatoes and a clutch of wild mushrooms. "Put these on skewers and roast them, if you will," he said.

Arthur nodded matter-of-factly. He was about ten. The only person he had ever known was Merlin. They had been together for as long as he could remember. He must have had a mother, but her face didn't register in his memory, not even dimly.

The old man with the flowing white beard had claimed his right to the royal baby only hours after it was born.

"I am the last keeper of the wizard's way," Merlin said. "And perhaps you will be the last to learn it." Setting the skewers on the fire, Arthur looked over his shoulder. He was intrigued now. Merlin a wizard? It had never occurred to him. The two lived alone in the forest and the crystal cave. The glow of the cave gave them their light. Arthur had learned to swim by turning into a fish. When he wanted food it appeared, or Merlin handed him some. Wasn't that how it was for everyone?

"You see, you will be leaving here soon," Merlin continued. "Mind you don't drop that potato in the ashes." Of course the boy already had. Because Merlin lived backward in time, his warnings inevitably came too late, after some minor disaster had already occurred. Arthur brushed the soot off the potato and replaced it on its skewer, made from the green wood of a linden tree.

"Never mind," Merlin said. "That one can be yours."

"What do you mean, leave?" Arthur asked. He had only been to the nearby village on rare occasions, when Merlin wanted to go to market, and at those times the wizard had been careful to disguise both of them in heavy, hooded cloaks. Yet the boy had been a keen observer, and what he had seen of other people troubled him.

Merlin gave his disciple a peculiar, squinting look. "I'm sending you into the swamp, or, as mortals call it, the world. I have kept you out of the swamp for all these years, teaching you something you are not to forget."

Merlin paused for effect, then said, "The way of the wizard."

After he uttered these words, neither spoke, as longtime companions are wont to do. They almost breathed the same breath, the old man and the boy, so Merlin must have sensed the restlessness that paced around inside Arthur's mind like a caged panther.

They ate their meal, and the boy went to wash in the azure pool downslope from the cave. When he came back Merlin was sunning himself on a favorite rock (*sunning* being a relative term —the quilted clouds had parted just enough to allow a single sunbeam to pierce the treetops and land upon the wizard's white hair). The first words out of the boy's mouth were "What will happen to you?"

"Me? Don't puff yourself up. I shall get along perfectly well without your help, thank you." The instant Merlin loosed this curt retort, he knew he had hurt the boy's feelings. But wizards are loath to apologize. A handsome, long bow made of white ash appeared on the ground beside Arthur, who picked it up eagerly and began to string it. In their private code, he knew that this was the old man's form of apology.

14

"What I am worried about is not myself," Merlin went on, "but the loss of knowledge. As I said, you may be the last to learn the way of the wizard."

"Then I will make sure it isn't lost," Arthur promised.

Merlin nodded. He did not speak of the wizard's way for the rest of that day or for many days thereafter. One morning in June, however, Arthur awoke to find his bed of pine boughs covered in snow. He shivered and sat up, scattering a cloud of white flakes into the air as he shook his deerskin blanket.

"I thought you only did this in December," he said, but Merlin did not reply. He was standing stock-still in the middle of the circle of snow that covered their camp. Before him was a strange apparition—a large boulder with a sword sticking out of it. Despite the chill in the air, none of the white snow clung to the stone, and the blade rose clean into the air, five feet of gleaming hammered damascene steel.

"What is that?" Arthur asked. The sight of the stone stirred him deeply, though he didn't know why.

"Nothing," replied Merlin. "Just remember it."

After a moment the sword in the stone began to fade, and by the time Arthur returned from his morning washup, Merlin's glade was warm again, every flake of snow had melted in the summer sun, and the stone had vanished like a dream. The boy felt like crying, for he knew that the apparition was Merlin's gesture of farewell, of farewell and remembrance.

What happened to Arthur after he went out into the world is by now the stuff of legend. He eventually found himself in London on a snowy Christmas morning outside the cathedral where the sword in the stone had mysteriously reappeared. To the astonishment of the crowd emerging from church, he pulled the sword out and claimed his right to be king. He fought long, bitter wars to overcome a horde of rivals to the throne, then established Camelot as his seat of power. Every day he lived the secrets of the wizard's way. Eventually he died and passed into history. It was left for later generations to wonder what Merlin

15

had taught his pupil all those years in the forest, before the boy Arthur stepped up to the stone and seized destiny by its jeweled hilt.

After Camelot fell, it took very little time for Arthur's world to be swept away. The land sank back into strife and ignorance, and Merlin proved to have been the last of his kind, just as he predicted. No more wizards appear in Western history after him.

But Merlin never thought that the way of the wizard depended on how history turned out. "What I know is in the air," he liked to say. "Breathe and it will be there." Wizards knew timeless things, and the storehouse of their knowledge therefore has to be outside time. The path is open. It begins everywhere and leads nowhere, yet it leads to a real place. All this unfolds as we listen to Merlin speak.

Lesson 1

✦

*A wizard exists in all of us. This wizard sees
and knows everything.*

*The wizard is beyond opposites of light and dark,
good and evil, pleasure and pain.*

*Everything the wizard sees has its roots
in the unseen world.*

Nature reflects the moods of the wizard.

*The body and the mind may sleep,
but the wizard is always awake.*

The wizard possesses the secret of immortality.

"Here," Merlin said one day, thrusting a bowl of soup at the boy Arthur. "Taste."

Hesitantly, Arthur did. It was a delicious potage of venison and wild roots mysteriously spiced by Merlin when Arthur's back was turned. In fact, the soup was irresistibly good, and Arthur eagerly dipped his spoon again, only to have the bowl snatched from his hands.

"Wait, more," he mumbled, his mouth still full. Merlin shook his head. "The whole banquet is in the first spoonful," he admonished.

At first Arthur felt a surge of frustration and disappointment, but then he noticed that he felt as satisfied as if he'd eaten the whole thing. Later, when Arthur was dozing under a tree, Merlin quietly approached and left a large bowl of soup by his side. Walking away, the wizard muttered, "Just remember, what good would all those years of wizard school be if I couldn't show you everything in the first lesson?"

UNDERSTANDING THE LESSON

It takes a lifetime to learn what the wizard has to teach, but everything that will unfold over years and decades is available in Merlin's first lesson. Here the wizard introduces himself. He describes his approach to life, which is to solve the deepest riddles of mortality and immortality. And all this happens in a magical way. For one thing, Merlin does not actually appear in physical form. Forms are irrelevant to Merlin. He has seen worlds come and go, he has survived the upheaval of aeons, and his reaction to everything is the same: he sees.

Wizards are seers. What do they see? Reality as a whole, not in its many parts.

"Were you always a wizard?" the boy Arthur asked.

"How could I have been?" replied Merlin. "I once walked around like you, and when I looked at a person, all I saw was a form of flesh and bones. But after a while I noticed that a person lives in a house that extends that body—unhappy people with messy emotions live in messy houses; happy, contented people live in orderly houses. It was a simple observation, but after a while I thought, When I see a house, I am actually seeing more of that person.

"Then my vision got wider. When I saw a person, I also couldn't help seeing her family and friends. These were also extensions of the person that told me much about who she really was. And still my vision expanded. I began to see beneath the mask of physical appearance. I saw emotions, desires, fears, wishes, and dreams. Certainly these are part of a person too, if you have eyes to see them.

"I began to observe the energy each person emanates. By this time the physical arrangement of flesh and bones had become almost insignificant, and soon I saw worlds within worlds in

18

everyone I encountered. Then I realized that every living thing is the entire universe, only wearing a different disguise."

"Is that really possible?" Arthur asked.

"A day will come when you will realize that the entire universe can be found inside you, and then you will be a wizard. As a wizard you don't live in the world, the world lives in you.

"Century after century the wizard has been sought out wherever he lived—in deep forests or caves, towers or temples. The wizard also has traveled under different names—philosopher, magician, seer, shaman, guru. 'Tell us why we suffer. Tell us why we grow old and die. Tell us why we are too weak to bring about a good life for ourselves.' Only to a wizard could mortals unburden themselves of so many difficult questions.

"After listening very carefully, the wizards, masters, and gurus all said the same thing. 'I can solve all this mass of ignorance and pain if you understand one thing. I am inside you. This separate person you seem to be talking to isn't separate. We are one, and at the level where we are one, none of your problems exists.' "

When Arthur once lamented that Merlin kept him in the forest with only brief glimpses of the world, Merlin snorted. "The world? How do you suppose those people live, the ones you've seen in the village? They worry about pleasure and pain, seeking the one and desperately avoiding the other. Being alive, they waste life worrying about death. Becoming rich or poor obsesses them constantly and feeds off their deepest fears."

Fortunately, the wizard within does not experience any of this. Because he sees the truth, he does not see untruth, for the play of opposites—pleasure and pain, rich and poor, good and evil—only seems real until you learn to see within the wizard's larger framework. Yet there is no denying that this drama of daily life is very real for ordinary people. The outer show of life *is* life if all you believe are your senses, what you see and feel.

Mortals turned to wizards to solve this obsession with appearances and this longing for meaning. There must be something more than we are living, mortals thought, not knowing exactly what that something more might be. "Spend time pondering not *what* you see," Merlin advised Arthur, "but *why* you see it."

The first lesson, then, comes down to this: look beyond your limited self to see your unlimited self. Pierce the mask of mortality and find the wizard. He is inside you and only there. Once you find him, you will also be a seer. But what you can see dawns in its own time, step by step. Before the seeing comes the feeling that there is more to life than what you are living. It's like a faint voice that whispers, "Find me." The voice that calls is unemotional, peaceful, content within itself—and elusive. It is the wizard's voice, but it is also your own.

LIVING WITH THE LESSON

Merlin's sayings work subtly, like water seeping deep into the earth. The water springing out of the ground today fell as rain thousands, even millions of years ago. No one knows much about the life of this hidden water, where it goes, what happens to it among the deep-hidden stones. But one day, released by gravity, it rises out of darkness, and, amazingly, the water springs up completely pure and fresh.

So it is with Merlin. If you sit in silence and listen for a few minutes, the words will begin to sink in. Let that happen, then let the wisdom do its work. Don't expect or anticipate any result, but be alert to whatever happens. Whatever happens is good.

This first lesson is about finding the wizard and appreciating his point of view, which is very different from the point of view adopted by either the mind or the emotions. Emotions feel and react. They are immediate, like the twitching arms of a sea anemone instantly responding to sensation. Pain causes emotional contraction; pleasure causes you to expand and feel liberated.

The mind, on the other hand, works much less immediately. It keeps a vast index file of memories and constantly shuffles through them. It compares the new with the old and renders a decision:

this is good, that is bad, this is worth repeating, that is not. Thus the emotions give an immediate, unthinking response to any situation, like a baby that smiles or cries spontaneously. The mind consults its memory bank and gives a delayed reaction.

The wizard does not have either of these reactions, immediate or delayed—Merlin simply is. He sees the world and allows it to be whatever it is. This isn't a passive act, however. The basis of everything in the wizard's world rests upon the insight "All this is myself." Therefore, in accepting the world as it is, the wizard views everything in the light of self-acceptance, which is the light of love.

It seems strange that the wizard's definition of love is wrapped up in silence. To the emotions, love is a surge of feeling, a very active attraction to some overwhelming stimulus. The mind has its own ways, but they are not so different: the mind loves whatever repeats a pleasurable experience from the past. "I love this" basically means "I love repeating what felt so good before." Thus both the mind and the emotions are selective. Picking and choosing isn't wrong, but it takes effort. Although we have all been taught that effort is good, that nothing is achieved without work, this isn't so. Being cannot be achieved by effort; love cannot be achieved by effort.

On a more subtle level, picking and choosing also involves rejection. The mind focuses on one thing at a time. Before you can say, "I like that," you have to reject all other choices. The things we reject tend to be colored by fear. The mind and emotions don't regard pain and suffering neutrally; they fear and reject them. This habit of picking and choosing winds up expending a lot of energy, because your mind is constantly vigilant, constantly watching out to make sure that hurt, disappointment, loneliness, and a great many other painful experiences don't happen again. What room is left for silence?

Without silence, there is no room for the wizard. Without silence, there cannot be any real appreciation of life, which is as delicate in its inner fabrics as a closed rosebud. When mortals

21

came to ask advice from the wizards, they did so because they noticed that wizards don't live in fear. Whatever happens to wizards is accepted, even embraced. "How do you manage this peace of mind?" mortals asked. And the wizards' answer was "Look within, where there is only peace."

So the first step into Merlin's world is to recognize that it exists—that is enough. As you sit with this lesson, your mind may rebel, saying "No!" to the very notion that there is another valid viewpoint, a way other than its own. Your emotions may join in this wave of mistrust, anxiety, boredom, skepticism, contempt—whatever may arise. Don't resist these feelings. They are merely old, habitual ways of picking and choosing. Your mind makes itself important by rejecting. For years it has faithfully served you, keeping unpleasant things at bay. The question is, Did the mind's tactics work? The mind may succeed in making you intelligent, but it is poorly equipped to make you happy, fulfilled, at peace with yourself.

Merlin doesn't argue with the mind. All debates are generated by thinking, and the wizard doesn't think. He sees. And that is the key to the miraculous, for whatever you can see in your inner world you will bring into existence in the outer world. Live with this first lesson, let the water of wisdom begin to seep into the secret passages inside your being, and observe. The wizard is inside you, and he wants only one thing: to be born.

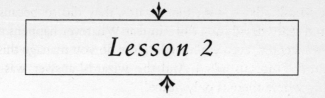

Lesson 2

The return of the magical can only happen with the return of innocence.

The essence of the wizard is transformation.

Every morning young Arthur went down to a pool in the forest to wash. Being a typical boy, he wasn't eager to perform this task. He was often distracted by chattering red squirrels, magpies, or anything that might be more interesting than soap and water.

Merlin did not bother too much about the dirt that visibly gathered all over his charge's face, around his neck, and everywhere else. But the day finally came when the wizard burst out, "I could plant beans behind your ears! It doesn't matter if you spend only a moment at the pool, but do something there."

Arthur hung his head. "I've been afraid to confess it, Merlin, but when I bend over the water, I can't see my own reflection. I can't see where to wash, or even what I look like."

To the boy's astonishment, when he looked up Merlin was beside himself with delight. "Here," he said, plunking a large emerald into the boy's hand as a reward (Arthur later used it to skip across the water). "I thought your disobedience marked a loss of innocence, but I see I was wrong. Having no reflection, you have no self-image. When you're not distracted by self-image, you can only be in the state of innocence."

UNDERSTANDING THE LESSON

Innocence is our natural state, before it becomes covered over. What covers it over is self-image. When we look at ourselves, even when we're trying to be completely honest, we see an

23

image built up over many years, in layers that are complexly woven together. The lines and wrinkles that develop in a person's face tell the story of past happiness and sadness, triumph and defeat, ideals and experiences. It is almost impossible to see anything else.

The wizard sees himself everywhere he looks because his sight is innocent. It is unclouded by judgments, labels, and definitions. A wizard still knows that he has an ego and a self-image, but he's not distracted by these things. He sees them against the backdrop of the totality, the whole context of life.

Ego is "I"; it is your singular point of view. In innocence this point of view is pure, like a clear lens. But without innocence the ego's focus is extremely distorting. If you think you know something—including yourself—you are actually seeing your own judgments and labels. The simplest words we use to describe each other—such as *friend, family, stranger*—are loaded with judgments. The enormous gulf in meaning between *friend* and *stranger,* for example, is filled with interpretations. A friend is treated one way, an enemy another. Even if we do not bring these judgments to the surface, they cloud our vision like dust obscuring a lens.

Because he has no labels for things, the wizard sees them afresh. For him there is no dust on the lens, so the world sparkles with newness. The same faint song is heard in everything: "Behold yourself." God could be defined as someone who looks around and sees only Him- or Herself in all directions; insofar as we are created in His/Her image, our world is also a looking glass.

Mortals found this wizardly viewpoint very strange, for their interest was drawn in an entirely different direction. They looked outward and were fascinated by things, and whatever thing they saw, they craved to name and then to use. Names had to be given to all the birds and beasts. Plants were to be grown for food or pleasure. Lands existed to be explored and conquered.

Merlin showed almost no interest in any of this. Wizards often do not know names for the most ordinary things, like oak trees, fallow deer, or the constellations. However, a wizard could look at a gnarled oak, a feeding doe, or the night sky for hours, and every moment of his contemplation would be all-absorbing.

Mortals wanted to share this kind of rapt attention. When asked the secret of how to look at the world afresh, with delighted eyes, Merlin said, "You lack innocence. Having labeled a thing, you no longer see that thing, you see its label instead." This was easy enough to illustrate. If two knights who were strangers met in the forest, they immediately searched for the emblem or pennant that told them whether the other was friend or foe. The instant this sign was spied, the knights could act, but only then. A friend could be embraced, welcomed to the feast, invited to tell stories. A foe could only be fought with.

This obsession to label things, Merlin said, is the activity of mind, pure and simple. Mind cannot react without a label. We carry millions of labels in our heads, and our minds can run through these labels with lightning swiftness. The speed of the mind is dazzling, but speed does not save us from staleness. Whatever you can think about, you have already experienced, and whatever you have already experienced, you are going to grow tired of. "Do you wonder that you cannot look at an oak or a deer or a star for more than a minute?" he said. "I can hear your minds all but groaning, 'That old thing!' and off you go on your mad rush for something new."

"I don't see why that's such a problem," one village elder said. "The world is vast, and nature is full of fascinating aspects and transformations."

"That is true enough," Merlin acknowledged, "but, by your argument, nothing should ever be stale and boring. The infinity of things *out there* can't be denied. But boredom is a common complaint among mortals, isn't that so?" The elder nodded.

"You have uttered the right word, however," Merlin went on. "*Transformation*. But it is your self that must constantly be transforming. You cannot bring the same stale self to the world and expect the world to be new for you."

The wizard never sees the same thing twice in the same way.

Thus, staring in the forest, he isn't absorbed so much in the sight of a deer as he is in some new facet of its being: gentleness, grace, shyness, or delicacy. When the eye is fresh, anyone can see these qualities. They unfold like petals of a rose. You must be patient, yet they are worth waiting for. Your own innocence is the only flower that exists. It never fades, and because of that, the world never fades either.

LIVING WITH THE LESSON

After you have read this lesson, give yourself a moment to try to regain a touch of innocence. This is easier than people imagine. The first thing to know is what *not* to do. Do not judge your present state of being. You may be tired or depressed. You may have a lot of anger or fear or blame to cast. Forget all this for a moment, because innocence, as Merlin teaches, is beyond the mind.

Just look at this list of words:

Heavy
Light
Black
White
Sun
Moon

Taking each in turn, let yourself experience these qualities. It doesn't matter if you are the kind of person who summons up images instead of feelings, or concepts instead of concrete objects. Any approach will work. Did you notice that it is impossible for your mind to avoid some sensation of heavy, light, black, white, and so on? In fact, you couldn't even read the words without summoning up at least a faint taste of each quality.

It takes your participation for these qualities to exist. If your participation is innocent, then they will exist in a fresh, new way. This is how a painter sees. He looks upon a basket of fruit, a boat, a cloud, but instead of being the passive recipient of these

26

things, he creates them through seeing. He imbues them with his own spirit.

And so do we all, even in the simplest act of seeing an ordinary thing. This experience demonstrates that innocence cannot be lost, it can only be covered over. The secret to seeing innocently is seeing from a new viewpoint, *one that is not conditioned by what you expect to see.*

"If you could really see that tree over there," Merlin said, "you would be so astounded that you'd fall over."

"Really? But why?" asked Arthur. "It's just a tree."

"No," Merlin said. "It's just a tree in your mind. To another mind it is an expression of infinite spirit and beauty. In God's mind it is a dear child, sweeter than anything you can imagine."

As long as the mind can register the color, light, density, and feeling of the world, *it is perceiving itself.* The word *heavy* or *white* gives you a sensation inside that belongs only to you. There isn't any heaviness or whiteness "out there" without you to perceive it; no sight, sound, touch, taste, or smell exists except as a small flicker of your awareness. Send a camera to the moon, record all the craters and valleys, and bring the film back to earth. If there is no human to see that picture, it has no image on it, only chemicals that have reacted to a momentary arrangement of photons. The film is as dead as the moon itself. Merlin would say that if no one looks at the moon's image, there is no moon either.

Therefore it is tremendously important to look at the world innocently, because that is the only way the world has any life. Your eye is the life giver of everything it sees. Behind every molecule of existence there must be awareness and intelligence; otherwise the universe would be a random swirl of inert gases and dead stars, a void aching to receive the seed of birth. Without intelligence, there is no life, only activity. Every glance you give outside your window puts the seed of life into creation. That is why Merlin took his job of watching oaks and deer and stars very seriously. He didn't want them to die; he was a lover of life.

This lesson comes down to saying, "See innocently and you

will give life." That is the magical creed Merlin lived by. Mortals found it hard to grasp something so simple because it ran contrary to their deepest prejudice, which said, "The world comes first and me second." But we ourselves would not be alive if some innocent Being had not first seen us. That was the act that planted the seed of the whole universe, and it was an act of love. You will know your own innocence again when you can see the love that breathes within every iota of creation.

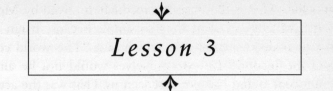

Lesson 3

*The wizard watches the world come and go,
but his soul dwells in realms of light.*

The scenery changes, the seer remains the same.

Your body is just the place your memories call home.

Merlin preferred to avoid the sight of mortals, but on a late summer eve he could occasionally be spotted standing on one foot at the edge of a field. Curious farmers would come up to him, but Merlin still stood like a statue, neither making a sound nor acknowledging their presence.

On such occasions Arthur thought his master looked like an old crane poised to spear fish in the marsh. One day, after Merlin had stared into a pond for several hours, the boy couldn't help asking what he was looking at.

"I cannot say exactly," replied Merlin. "I saw a dragonfly and wanted to look at it more closely. It flew across my path like a fluttering dream, but after a moment I forgot whether I was dreaming of this dragonfly or whether it was dreaming of me."

"Isn't the answer obvious?" Arthur asked.

Merlin gave the boy a sharp thump on the head. "You think your dreams exist here, inside. But I find myself everywhere, so who knows which part of me is dreaming another part?"

UNDERSTANDING THE LESSON

The wizard inside each of us could also be called the witness. The role of the witness is not to interfere in the changing world, but to see and understand. The witness doesn't rest—it remains

29

awake even when you are dreaming or in a dreamless sleep. It therefore does not need to see through your eyes, which seems quite magical. Isn't the eye the essential organ of sight?

Energy and information are basic to anything we can see, hear, or touch in the relative world—every atom can be broken down into these two components. Yet in their primordial state these ingredients are formless. A bundle of energy can drift away in a chaotic swirl like a puff of smoke; information can break down into random blips of data. It takes another force to organize the wondrous order of life—intelligence. Intelligence is the glue of the universe.

To the wizard, this isn't just a theoretical notion, because he can see with his own inner eye that *he is that intelligence.* Mortals are baffled by such understanding, since it isn't of the mind. They are used to knowing things, but not used to *knowingness* itself. "The most brilliant mortal," Merlin said, "is no better than the greatest fool as soon as both go to bed. They dream the same fearful nightmares and worry about dying. Fear is born with them, and they cannot enjoy the slightest pleasure without knowing that it will fade away."

The wizard's knowingness remains present even in sleep. Awake, ever-conscious, all-knowing, universal intelligence is to the wizard not some distant creative force. It lives in every atom. It is the eye behind the eye, the ear behind the ear, the mind behind the mind.

So it isn't necessary for the wizard to be awake with his eyes open to see. Seeing in its deepest sense can take place while we dream or sleep, because to see means to be awake to the universe's intelligence. When the witness is fully present, everything is understood.

The wizard's knowledge is pure knowingness without reliance on external facts. It is the water of life tapped directly from the source. No matter what sorts of changes sweep across the universe, the wizard's knowingness cannot change—the scenery comes and goes, the seer remains the same. Before we encounter the wizard inside us, we all depend on our senses and our minds to know what we know. Ours is a learned knowledge. It is stored in memory and cataloged according to what interests us; it is therefore selective. The wizard's knowledge is innate.

One time Arthur was scared out of his wits when Merlin ran around brandishing a huge butcher's knife like a madman. "What are you doing?" the boy asked in terror.

"Thinking," Merlin replied. "Don't you think this way?"

"No," Arthur said.

Merlin suddenly stopped. "Ah, then I must be mistaken. My impression was that all mortals used their minds like knives, cutting and dissecting. I wanted to see what that was like. If I may say so, there is a good deal of violence hidden in what you mortals call rationality."

The wizard's mind is like a lens that gathers in what it sees and lets everything pass through without distortion. The advantage of this kind of awareness is that it unites, whereas the rational mind separates. The rational mind looks "out there" at a world of objects in time and space, whereas the wizard sees everything as part of himself. In place of "out there" and "in here," there is only one seamless flow.

Hence Merlin's claim that he could hardly tell if he was dreaming of a dragonfly or the dragonfly was dreaming of him. Only in separation, as seen by the mind, was there a difference. In the wizard's eye, both were one.

LIVING WITH THE LESSON

It isn't easy to explain what witnessing is. In an ordinary waking state, we all see objects, but the witness sees *light*. It sees itself as one focus of light, the object as another, all in the context of a vast, changing realm of nothing but light.

Light is a metaphor for higher states of being. When someone has a near-death experience and says, "I went into the light," she means that she experienced a finer degree of herself.

The light may take on the image of heaven or another world, but to the wizard our ordinary world is also only an image. It too is projected from awareness.

"All awareness is light," Merlin said, "all light is awareness." The boundaries we erect to divide heaven from earth, mind from matter, real from unreal are mere conveniences. Having made the boundaries, we can unmake them just as easily.

Look at this page carefully. You see it as an object. It is solid insofar as it is made of wood fibers turned into paper, but it is abstract in that it is made of ideas. Is a page a thing of paper, a thing of ideas, or both? Notice how easily you can see it as both, but also notice that you cannot see both at the same time. Different realities can coexist, in other words, but each respects its own level of being. A word is just ink dots at one level, but it is the key to an idea on another.

Every state of being, from the finest and most immaterial to the grossest and most solid, depends on the observer. If we wanted to, we could dissolve the solid page into nothingness, as follows: a page is made of paper, paper is made of molecules, molecules are made of atoms, atoms are bundles of energy at the quantum level, and bundles of energy consist of 99.99999 percent empty space. Since the distance between one atom and the next is quite vast—proportionally greater than the distance between the earth and the sun—you can call this page solid only if you are also willing to say that the space between us and the sun is solid.

This experience of turning solid-seeming things into nothingness can also be reversed. Starting with "empty" space, you can build energy bundles, atoms, molecules, and so on up the chain of creation until you arrive at any object you want, including your own body. The hand turning this page is a cloud of energy, and the only way you can feel your hand or it can feel the page is through an act of awareness. Other energy bundles, such as the ultraviolet light surrounding you, totally escape your notice. Thus the world's comings and goings are entirely dependent upon the power of perception. You were created as a seer in order for the world to exist as a thing to be seen. Without eyes, the world would be invisible.

Now we can take this understanding and go a step further. Everything on earth is nourished by the sun, which is just a star. The food you eat was converted from starlight, and as you eat it you create a body that has the same source. In other words, your eating a meal is just the act of starlight taking in starlight. This light, although it assumes many forms, from swirling gases and quasars to a rabbit nibbling clover, is just one light. It has no location but is everywhere. You seem to have a location, but that is true only because you are right now engaging in the supremely creative act of turning the universe of light into a single focus called your body and mind.

"I'd like to perform miracles," Arthur begged one day.

"This world exists because of you," replied Merlin. "Isn't that miracle enough?"

The wizard takes this magical reasoning to the ultimate. If sight made the world visible, he asks, who or what is the creator of sight? Who saw the eye before the eye saw anything? The answer is awareness. The seer behind the eye is just consciousness itself, giving birth to our senses so that they can give birth to everything around us.

This isn't a metaphysical mystery. Inside a mother's womb the embryo is born as a single cell with no senses; then it evolves into multiple cells that clump into specific regions that concentrate on various functions; and eventually those functions emerge as eyes, ears, tongue, nose, and so on. An eye does not look at all like an ear, but their different forms are deceptive. All of your senses were contained in that first fertilized cell in the form of coded information.

Information is just awareness made manifest in storable form —like this book. If you didn't know what a book was, you'd say it was simply a collection of marks in some strange code, when in fact it is a channel for one awareness to communicate with another.

In Merlin's view, the whole world was a way for him to talk to himself. "If you ever forget anything," he advised Arthur, "the forest will remind you."

"I've forgotten lots of things the forest didn't remind me about," the boy protested.

"Not true," replied Merlin. "The only thing you can forget is yourself, and it can be found under every tree."

Why does the world exist? Because one vast consciousness wanted to write the code of life and unfold its strands across the page of time. It is no wonder that a wizard cannot tell where his own body ends and the world begins. Are you dreaming this book, or is this book dreaming you?

*Who am I? is the only question worth asking
and the only one never answered.*

*It is your destiny to play an infinity of roles,
but these roles are not yourself.*

*The spirit is nonlocal, but it leaves behind a fingerprint,
which we call the body.*

*A wizard does not believe himself to be a local event
dreaming of a larger world.
A wizard is a world dreaming of local events.*

Merlin disappeared from Arthur's world for many years; then one day he suddenly reappeared, walking out of the forest and up to Camelot. Overjoyed to see his master, King Arthur ordered a royal banquet in his honor. But Merlin acted bewildered, looking at his former pupil as if he had never seen him before.

"Perhaps I might attend, if you are who I take you to be," Merlin said. "But tell me truly, who are you?" Arthur was astonished, but before he could protest, Merlin addressed the assembled court, saying loudly, "I shall offer this bag of gold dust to anyone who can tell me who this person is." And immediately a purse bulging with pure dust of gold appeared in his hands.

Baffled and chagrined, none of the Round Table knights came forward. Then a young page ventured, "We all know this is the king." Merlin shook his head and curtly dismissed the page from the hall.

"Don't any of you know who this is?" he repeated.

"It is Arthur," another voice called out. "Even a fool knows that." Merlin spotted where the voice came from—an old serving maid in the corner—and ordered her from the room too. The whole court buzzed with confusion, but soon the wizard's challenge turned into a game.

Various answers began to fly: the son of Uther Pendragon, ruler of Camelot, sovereign of England. Merlin accepted none of them, nor the more ingenious answers, such as son of Adam, flower of Albion, a man among men, and so on. Eventually Guinevere herself was drawn in. "This is my beloved husband," she murmured. Merlin only shook his head. One by one, each person was dismissed until no one remained in the great hall but the wizard and the king.

"Merlin, you have stymied us all," Arthur admitted. "But I am sure I know who I am. Therefore my answer is this: I am your old friend and disciple." After the briefest of hesitations, Merlin dismissed this last answer as he had all the others, and the king himself had no choice but to leave. Curiosity, however, led him to an open door from which he could still see into the great hall. To his surprise, he watched Merlin walk over to a casement window, open the purse, and fling the gold dust into the air.

"Why did you throw away that precious gold?" Arthur called out, unable to contain himself.

Merlin looked up. "I had to," he replied. "The wind told me who you are."

"The wind? But it didn't say anything."

"Exactly."

UNDERSTANDING THE LESSON

Wizards and their kind have often been content to remain nameless and placeless. They do not like to stay in any one locale where mortals might become overfamiliar. "Whoever calls my name is a stranger," Merlin said. "Your recognizing my face doesn't mean you know me."

36

Wizards see themselves as citizens of the cosmos. Therefore any localized place where they can be found is irrelevant.

In mortal life what limits us first and last are names, labels, and definitions. Having a name is useful—it lets you know which birth certificate is yours—but it quickly turns into a limitation. Your name is a label. It defines you as having been born at such and such a time and place to a certain set of parents. After a few years your name defines you as going to such and such a school, then on to such and such a profession. By the time you are thirty, your identity is hemmed in by a box of words. The walls of the box might consist of the following: "Catholic tax lawyer, educated at Cornell, married with three children and a mortgage." These facts may not be inaccurate, but they are misleading. They trap an unconditioned spirit inside conditions.

Many of these limitations seem to pertain to *you* when in fact they only pertain to your body—and you are far more than your body. The wizard has a peculiar relationship to his body. He sees it as a wisp of consciousness taking shape in the world, much as rocks, trees, mountains, words, wishes, and dreams flow and take shape. The fact that a wish or a dream is insubstantial, while one's body is solid, does not perturb a wizard. Wizards lack our ordinary prejudice that equates "solid" with "real."

A wizard does not believe himself to be a local event dreaming of a larger world. A wizard is a world dreaming of local events. No boundaries restrict him. Mortals could not exist without boundaries. Their bodies define where they are—without a body, one could not even know where home is, since home is where the body goes to find shelter and rest.

Merlin did not consider himself homeless, however. He said, "This body is like a roost that my thoughts come home to, but they fly in and out so fast that you might as well say they live in the air." Again, we assume that thoughts come and go inside our heads, but we cannot prove it. Who has seen a thought before it arises? Who follows a thought wherever it chances to go next?

Merlin could not understand why mortals wanted to cling to

their bodies. "It is well enough to say that this package of flesh and bones is 'me,' " he said, "but only if that hill and that pasture and that castle are also 'me.' " A mortal body was no better, in Merlin's eyes, than a coat rack on which beliefs, fears, prejudices, and dreams were left hanging. If you hang too many coats on a rack, you cannot see the rack anymore. This is what mortals have done with their bodies, Merlin said. It is impossible to see the truth of the human body—that it is a river of awareness flowing through time—because so much weight of the past has accumulated on it.

LIVING WITH THE LESSON

To experience this lesson, you need to forget your name for a while. Let's say that Who am I? is a real question now. Escaping name and form means finding out who you really are. Most of the time we experience ourselves through limitation. Playing a role is a limitation, yet every person slips in and out of roles all the time. Remember when you were a child and your mother was all-important. It did not occur to you that she had a life other than being Mommy; her identity was fixed in your mind. Only after you grew up did you see that she played other roles, such as wife, sister, daughter, career woman, and so on. It is difficult for most children to accept the fact that mothers live lives that are not centered entirely around motherhood—such is the natural self-centeredness of all small children. But over time we learn to slip into our own roles by following the examples of our parents.

Taking on more roles seems like a way of expanding our experience. A woman who was only a mother would find her life suffocating. Being "complete" in our society means wearing as many hats as possible. But the wizard does not see the situation that way at all. To him being complete means being free from all roles. "I am a free spirit reduced to the appearance of this little body," Merlin would say. "You can circle the sun with your thumb and forefinger, but doesn't its light still fill the sky?"

Stepping out of role playing is a tricky business, yet you cannot enter the wizard's world if you define yourself through the roles you play. So what is the experience of being entirely free from roles? It is actually quite simple. When you wake up in the morning, there is an instant before you start thinking about your day, a moment of just feeling awake without any particular thought on your mind. You are just yourself, in a simple state of awareness. This experience of simplicity repeats itself off and on during the day, but few people notice it, because our habit is to identify with the thinking process. It too goes on throughout the day. In reality, however, *you are not what you are thinking*.

You may find this hard to believe, but the thoughts in your head don't belong to you—they belong to your name, to the roles you have slipped into. If you are a woman thinking about her child, how he is doing in school, what to make him for dinner, and so on, *you* are not having these thoughts. *Mother* is. If in my medical practice I go around thinking about diagnoses, prescriptions, and so on, *Doctor* is having those thoughts. Mother and doctor are useful roles, of course, but they come to an end, and one day each of us is faced with the riddle Who am I? which never got answered, no matter how well we played our roles.

You can slip beyond roles in a split second if you want to, however. As you read this page, turn your attention to the one who is doing the reading. Or while listening to music, turn to the one who is hearing. Or if you happen to see a rainbow, catch sight of the one who is seeing. In all these cases you will immediately sense an awareness that is alert, awake, uninvolved, silent, yet intensely alive. What have you actually done? You have interrupted the act of observation to catch a glimpse of the observer. This trick gives insight into an absolute certainty of your existence, for beyond all observation lies the unchanging observer. This seer is the timeless factor in every time-bound experience, and this seer is you.

To be timeless can be a frightening prospect if you are

strongly identified with your role playing. Countless people are devastated when they lose their jobs, when their children grow up and leave home, when a beloved spouse dies. Their sense of "I" is so bound up in names, labels, and roles that they haven't made time to find out who they really are.

Being fully human makes us real. Reality can't be defined, it can only be experienced. Be alert to those brief moments during the day when you experience your fundamental self behind a breath, a feeling, a sensation. Before you jump out of bed tomorrow, see if you can catch the fleeting hint of being, pure and simple, before the mind starts chattering. This still, silent, nameless state is very satisfying. It cannot be touched by thinking, talking, or doing. It's the castle whose walls no army will ever scale, guarding the treasure house where the real riches of life are stored.

Lesson 5

Wizards don't believe in death.
In the light of awareness, everything is alive.

There are no beginnings or endings.
To the wizard these are only mental constructs.

To be most fully alive, you have to be dead to the past.

Molecules dissolve and pass away, but consciousness
survives the death of the matter on which it rides.

Every story about Merlin, even the most confused, took it for granted that he lived backward in time. In his day this caused much consternation among mortals. The old wizard would shout "Watch it!" the second *after* Arthur spilled boiling water on himself. He would pop up at funerals and chuck the corpse under the chin as if it were a newborn baby. If that wasn't strange enough, the villagers whispered that Merlin had been seen in graveyards handing out christening presents to the headstones.

"Can you explain why you live backward in time?" the boy Arthur once asked.

"Because all wizards do," replied Merlin.

"And why is that?"

"Because we choose to. It has many advantages."

"I don't see any," Arthur persisted, thinking of Merlin's strange habits, such as eating breakfast before he went to bed.

"Here, I will show you," Merlin said, taking Arthur outside the crystal cave. It was a hot summer day with the sun straight overhead and the wild roses drooping almost to the ground.

"Now," Merlin said, handing the boy a shovel, "begin digging a ditch from here to there, and don't stop until I tell you."

Arthur pitched into his task, digging with all his might, but after an hour he was exhausted, and still Merlin had not told him to stop. "Is this long enough?" he asked. Merlin regarded the ditch, which was perhaps ten feet long and two feet deep.

"Yes, quite sufficient," he said. "Now fill it up again."

Accustomed as he was to obeying, Arthur did not like this order very much. Sweating and grim faced, he toiled under the blazing sun until the ditch was entirely filled again.

"Now sit beside me," said Merlin. "What did you think of that work you did?"

"It was pointless," Arthur blurted out.

"Exactly, and so is most human effort. But the pointlessness isn't discovered until too late, after the work has been done. If you lived backward in time, you would have seen ditch digging as pointless and not begun in the first place."

UNDERSTANDING THE LESSON

The legends of Arthurian times claiming that Merlin lived backward in time were a simplification. The old myth tellers loved to astonish, and any reader who tried to unriddle what living backward in time meant would marvel at the strange creature Merlin really was. As a result some took him for a prophet or a soothsayer. Any prophet could be said to live backward in time, since prophets seem to experience what has yet to happen.

But at a deeper level, to the medieval mind living backward in time meant defying the natural cycle of birth and death. Someone who grows younger every day has escaped the immutable laws that make all living things decay and die. A wizard's day of birth, it would seem, is the day he disappears from the world, assuming that he dies at all.

To unravel this paradox one has to understand time as a wizard experiences it. "You mortals took your name from death,"

Merlin said in the crystal cave. "You would be called immortals if you believed in yourselves as creatures of life."

"That's not fair," Arthur protested. "We didn't choose death. It was thrust upon us."

"No, you are simply used to it. All of you grow old and die because you see others grow old and die. Throw off this worn-out habit, and you will no longer be trapped in the net of time."

"Throw off death? How does one do that?" Arthur wanted to know.

"To begin with, go back to the source of your habit. There you will find some bit of false reasoning that convinced you to be mortal in the first place. False reasoning lies at the root of any false belief. Then find the flaw in your logic and pluck it out. It is all very simple."

Arthur passed into legend as the "once and future king," implying that he too had escaped the spell of death. What did he find? What is the false logic that wizards see behind mortality? Essentially it is our identification with the body. Human bodies are born, grow old, and die. Identifying with this process is false logic, but, once embraced, it dooms us to die as well. We fall under the spell of mortality and have no choice but to embrace death.

To break the spell requires a shift of identity from the time-bound to the timeless. Therefore the wizard sets out on a journey to discover the truth about time—this is the real meaning behind the tale that Merlin lived backward in time. He wanted to follow time back to its roots.

LIVING WITH THE LESSON

In the wizard's experience time is just quantified eternity. "All of us are surrounded by the timeless," Merlin claimed. "The question is, What do you do with it?" Cutting the timeless into little pieces creates time, and that is still our tendency. To us time flows by in linear fashion. Clocks tick away seconds, minutes, and hours, recording the long march from past to present to future. This linear conception of time was displaced by Einstein when he proved that time is relative, that it has the capacity to speed up or slow down.

Besides looking a bit like Merlin, Einstein must actually have slipped into the wizard's world to come up with this astonishing notion. He could *feel* the theory of relativity, Einstein tells us, long before he could prove it mathematically. We all feel time as a relative, fluid thing—any happy experience makes it speed up, any painful experience makes it slow down. A day in love seems like a second, a morning in the dentist's chair feels like an eternity.

But can this new perception of time really get us past death? To the wizard death is merely a belief. Relativity allows us to bend our belief in linear time. It isn't hard to think up other examples that would enable us to believe in immortality itself. For example, if you see the universe as a storehouse of energy, then from the viewpoint of energy, nothing ever dies, because energy cannot be destroyed. As energy you will always be here.

"But I don't want to be energy," Arthur protested when faced with this logic.

"That's your fatal flaw," Merlin pointed out. "Because you identify with this body, you think you need a form. Energy is formless, so you think it can't be you. But I was only pointing out that energy can't be born; it has no beginning or end. Until you stop thinking of yourself as having a beginning, you'll never find the deathless part of yourself, which must be unborn if it is never to die."

Seeing the boy's downcast face, Merlin said more reassuringly, "I'm not stealing your body to establish that you are formless. You only need to see the formless within the form, then you can have immortality in the midst of mortality."

Molecules form and dissolve, returning to the primordial soup of atoms. But consciousness survives the death of the molecules on which it rides. What was once a bundle of energy in a

44

sunbeam turns into a leaf, only to fall and change again into soil. This change of state crosses many boundaries. A sunbeam is invisible, whereas leaves and soil are visible. A leaf is alive and growing, whereas sunbeams aren't. The colors of light, leaf, and soil are different, and so on.

But all these transformations exist as constructs of the mind. The actual energy present in the sunbeam experiences no change at all—it is simply part of the constant play of photons and electrons that underlies everything, whether we perceive it as dead or alive. Modern science has already led our minds into the appropriate new perspective; now we have to learn to *live* it. Visionary thinkers such as Einstein can only help us overcome mental barriers; we have to break through the others, the emotional and instinctual barriers, ourselves.

The emotional fear of death is one such barrier. As wizards see it, the whole phenomenon of death is tied up in fear, although this fear is so deeply rooted that its effects are not immediately obvious. There is a simple exercise, however, for uncovering this for yourself. Sit with a stack of several sheets of paper. Choose a quiet room with no distractions. Now place the tip of your pen on the first sheet of paper and promise that you will not lift the pen for five minutes. Begin to write the sentence "I am afraid of" and finish it any way you like.

Not lifting your pen, write the same sentence opening, "I am afraid of," and again let any ending that comes to mind be put on the paper. As you are doing this, take slow, measured breaths in and out without pausing in between. This is sometimes called circular breathing, in which inhale and exhale are connected. Since ancient times this deliberate sort of breathing has been considered a way to bypass the inhibitions of the conscious mind. Without this technique, it would be much harder to reach the unconscious level of fear.

As you perform the circular breathing, in and out without pausing, keep finishing the same sentence, "I am afraid of," over and over again without lifting pen from paper. Once you liberate yourself to write down your hidden fears, you may find it difficult to stop.

If you are doing this exercise freely, letting your thoughts simply unravel without trying to control them, you will discover many strange and unanticipated associations with fear. And these unexpected fears will bring emotions with them, not just fear but anger, sorrow, and great relief. Pent-up tears may begin to flow.

Let all emerge, but always return to your breathing and don't lift the pen from the paper until you are done. One word of caution: if you begin to feel too uncomfortable, stop. At the end of this exercise, it is also a good idea to lie down and rest, allowing yourself to regain your normal equilibrium. I find that this exercise is most effective the first time, but it can be repeated whenever you wish.

What does this all have to do with the wizard's view of immortality? We might say that undertaking one five-minute session devoted to fear is like peeling away one layer of a belief system. Immortality is at the core of human life, but it is wrapped in layer after layer of contrary beliefs. These beliefs are actualized in daily life—we live our fears, wishes, dreams, unconscious associations, and ultimately our deepest belief that we must die. The rational mind would probably defend this stance by claiming that death is everywhere in nature.

But Merlin would say, "Look at your rational doubts more closely. Behind the doubt stands a doubter, behind the doubter a thinker, behind the thinker a speck of pure awareness that must be conscious before any thought can arise. I am that speck of consciousness. I am immortal and immune to time. Do not just speculate about me, judging whether to accept or reject. Dive inside, peel away your layers of doubt. When we finally meet, you will know who I am. And then my immortality will be not simply a notion but a living reality."

*The wizard's consciousness is a field
that exists everywhere.*

*The streams of knowledge contained in the
field are eternal and flow forever.*

*Centuries of knowledge are compressed
in revelatory moments.*

We live as ripples of energy in the vast ocean of energy.

*When the ego is set aside, you have access
to the totality of memory.*

One morning Arthur woke up very early, shivering in his straw bed, only to find Merlin looking at him from across the cave.

"I was having a bad dream," Arthur mumbled. "I was the last person left on earth, wandering forests and streets that were empty of anyone but me."

"Dream?" said Merlin. "That was no dream. You *are* the last person on earth."

"How can that be?" Arthur asked.

"Wouldn't you agree that the only person on earth would also have to be the last person?"

"Yes."

"Well, from the point of view of your self-image, which people in the future have called the ego, you are the only one."

"How can you say that? You and I are here together, aren't we? And we have visited villages and towns that must contain thousands of folk."

Merlin shook his head. "If you look at yourself truly, what are you? A creature of experience that is constantly turning into memories. When you say 'I,' you are indicating this unique bundle of experiences, with all its private history that no one else can share.

"Nothing seems more personal than memory. You and I have walked separate roads, even though we walk together. I cannot look at a flower without having an experience you do not share. Not a single tear or laugh can truly be given to another."

When Merlin had finished this speech, Arthur looked distressed. "You make it sound as if everyone is utterly alone," the boy said.

"Not I," replied Merlin. "The work of the ego is what makes you alone, sealing you into a world no one else can enter." Seeing how distraught his disciple looked, Merlin softened his voice. "And yet ego can be set aside. Come with me." He got up and led Arthur out of the cave into the predawn darkness, which was still full of stars.

"How far away is that star, do you suppose?" he asked, pointing to the Dog Star. It being midsummer, Sirius was bright and low on the horizon.

"I don't know. I suppose it must be farther than I can measure, or possibly imagine," Arthur replied.

Merlin shook his head. "It is no distance at all. Consider this: for you to see that star, its light must enter your eye, correct? Beams of light flow continuously from here to there, like an invisible bridge. What is a star but light? Therefore, if it is light both here and there and on the bridge in between, there is no separation between you and that star. You are both part of the same seamless field of light."

"But it appears to be very far away. After all, I can't pluck it out of the sky," Arthur objected.

Merlin shrugged. "Separation is only an illusion. You appear to be separate from me and from other people because your ego

48

takes the view that we are all isolated and alone. But I assure you, if you set your ego aside, you would see us all surrounded by one unending field of light, which is awareness. Your every thought is born in a vast ocean of light only to return to it, along with every cell of your body. This field of awareness is everywhere, an invisible bridge to all else that exists.

"So there is nothing about you that isn't part of everyone else —except as ego sees it. Your work is to go beyond ego and dive into the universal ocean of consciousness."

Arthur had a thoughtful look on his face. "I'll have to think about what you've said."

"You do that." Merlin yawned. "I'm still sleepy." The wizard turned to reenter the warm, snug cave. "Oh, and by the way, before you come back to bed, will you please hang that thing up again?"

"Thing?" Arthur looked down in surprise to see that the Dog Star had been plucked from the sky and left at his feet.

UNDERSTANDING THE LESSON

The ego has taken on the job of selecting and rejecting experiences, as we've already seen. As a result, the ego creates isolation, since anything that picks and chooses creates a gap. Between you and something you've rejected, there is a gap. Between you and me there is also a gap, because we have chosen not to have the same experience—our egos are separate.

In fact, we all take it for granted that we couldn't possibly share experiences, not fully. I cannot enter all of your emotions, fears, wishes, and dreams, nor you mine. The best we can usually do is to try to build bridges of communication, which often prove too weak to hold. The most personal things about you since you were born—your memories and experiences—lead to loneliness and isolation.

The wizard is never isolated, however, because ego does not

enter into his view of things. By *ego* is meant the sense of a personal, unsharable "I." Merlin once said to the boy Arthur, "Try to forget me if you can."

"What?" Arthur said in surprise. "I could never forget you—and I don't want to." He felt anxious, supposing that Merlin was rejecting him in some way. "Do you want to forget me?" he asked.

"Oh, absolutely," Merlin replied calmly. "You see, I want us to be friends, and if I remember you, what do I have? Not the real you, but a dead image. That is all a memory is, a once-living thing turned into a dead image. But as long as I can forget you every day, then I will wake up to see you anew the day after. I will see the real you, stripped of outworn images."

Setting ego aside means setting memory aside. When that is done, people are no longer isolated. The individual mind narrows our awareness down, as if we are looking at the world through a peephole. In the wizard's world, everyone shares the same universal consciousness. It flows forever and embraces all thoughts, all emotions, all experiences. "Insofar as you are one person," Merlin taught, "you are like a drop in the ocean. Insofar as you are a part of universal awareness, you are the whole ocean."

"Doesn't one drop simply melt away and get lost in the ocean?" Arthur asked.

"No—an individual can never be obliterated, even through the experience of the ocean of consciousness," Merlin assured him. "You can be yourself and be the All at the same time. That may seem a mystery, yet it is so."

LIVING WITH THE LESSON

We all cling to memory because it defines us. But to bring an end to separation and isolation, you have to be willing to see the unreality of memory. Think of someone you know well—your husband or wife, a sibling or friend. Bring him or her to your mind in detail and ask yourself what you really know about this person. Go beyond mere facts, such as eye color, weight, job, or address. Think instead about the most personal traits, likes and dislikes, vivid memories and interactions.

When you finish this exercise, you may assume that you have compiled an accurate portrait of that person. Yet everything you've recalled came from your memory, and therefore what you have described is your individual viewpoint. That same person could be described entirely differently from another perspective. What seems likable to you is unlikable to others, what is memorable to you may be entirely forgettable in someone else's eyes.

You do not have to go very far to realize that *everything* in your description is completely relative. Your idea of tall is someone else's idea of short or average, heavy can be seen as light, fair as dark, friendly as unfriendly, and so forth. You are really describing your perspective, not the person. Moreover, your experiences with that person are uniquely your own, which makes your description even more idiosyncratic. If everything you thought you knew about someone else has turned out to be indirectly about you, it is obvious that memory serves to isolate. We fragment the world by the personal way we view it, creating shells of isolation that no one else can penetrate, not fully.

Because it is completely relative, your viewpoint cannot be called real. Reality doesn't depend on a viewpoint—it simply is. And most of us, dwelling as we do inside our private worlds, do not contact the real very often. The unreal is the habitat of the senses; the real is the habitat of the wizard. You have to look behind the curtain of memory to begin to discover the true fabric of reality.

When the doors of perception are cleansed, you will begin to see the unseen world—the wizard's world.

There is a wellspring of life within you where you can go for cleansing and transformation.

Purification consists of getting rid of the toxins in your life: toxic emotions, toxic thoughts, toxic relationships.

All living bodies, physical and subtle, are bundles of energy that can be perceived directly.

One day, when Merlin and Arthur were both in a drowsy, summery mood lying beside a stream, Merlin said, "I read a poem as a boy, a long time in the future. I wonder if you will like it?" Arthur pretended he was asleep, covering his face with his hand to ward off the July sun. Whenever Merlin talked about the future as his past, the boy needed a good deal of concentration to follow him.

"You needn't try to ignore me," Merlin went on, "for this poem is too beautiful to neglect:

> "What if you slept,
> And what if,
> in your sleep
> you dreamed?
> And what if,
> in your dream,
> you went to heaven
> and there plucked

a strange and beautiful flower?
And what if,
when you awoke,
you had the flower
in your hand?
What then?"

UNDERSTANDING THE LESSON

When we are awake we keep our attention glued to the sights
and sounds of the material world, so it is easy to assume that the
physical body is the only body we have. What is a body? The
broadest definition would be a collection of cells working
together to form a larger unit. Being much greater than the sum
of its parts, a body can act and think and feel in ways impossible
for a single cell.

Let's apply this definition to an unexpected place—feelings.
Every day you have isolated feelings that are like single cells; put
them all together and you have your *emotional body*. Your emotional body is, first of all, a living history of all the things you like
and dislike, as well as your fears, hopes, desires, and so on. If your
emotional body could walk into the room, your friends would
recognize you immediately, since the emotional body gives us a
huge part of our identity.

There are other bodies, also invisible, that add to your
uniqueness. There is the body of knowledge that has been
growing with you since birth—call this your *mental body*.
Knowledge is subtler than emotions, since it is made up of
abstract concepts. But even subtler are all the reasons you have
for living, your deep beliefs about existence and the nature of
life—all stored within your *causal body*, that part of you that
allows you to understand existence. Here reside the deepest
seeds of memory and desire.

All of these bodies are unique to you. Again, if your mental
body or causal body could walk into a room, you would be

immediately identifiable. So *identity*—your feeling of being "I" —flows from your awareness of these bodies. A wizard knows that this glow moves from the subtlest body to the grossest. The "I" you identify with is created first by your beliefs and reason for living (causal body), which give rise to ideas (mental body) and feelings (emotional body). Only at the end of the sequence does the physical body receive the impulse of life. As Merlin said, "Mortals believe that they are physical machines that learned to think. Actually, they are thoughts that learned to create a physical machine."

LIVING WITH THE LESSON

In practical terms this knowledge has huge implications. If you assume that you are first and foremost a physical being, you will live your life totally differently from someone who assumes that he or she is first and foremost a subtle being.

Arthur and Merlin were coming home from a trek in the Questing Wode, the deep forest that was the wizard's domain. As usual Arthur was much more tired than Merlin after their exertions; he lay down under a tree to take a nap. No sooner had he closed his eyes, however, than he felt himself being poked in the ribs.

"What is it?" he grumbled drowsily. "Let me sleep."

Poking him again with a hazel switch, Merlin shook his head. "You need your strength for the last leg home. If you take a nap you'll be exhausted."

"Exhausted? That's why I'm trying to take a nap in the first place," replied Arthur.

"Ah, but you do much more work asleep than I've ever seen you do awake," Merlin said. He knew this would pique Arthur's curiosity, and, after a few tosses and turns on the soft grass under the tree, the boy sat up. "What kind of work do I do in my sleep? Why am I not aware of it?" he asked.

"Oh, all kinds of work," Merlin replied casually. "In your sleep your physical body rests and repairs itself. In dreams your emotional body carries out its wishes, fears, hopes, and fantasies. Your causal body returns to the world of light, which some people perceive as heaven. By others, however, it is perceived as the sudden solution to a problem or an insight that strikes out of the blue after they wake up. In all these ways you are resetting the intricate coordination among all your bodies.

"The most creative act you will ever undertake is this act of creating yourself. It takes place on countless levels, seen and unseen. It marshals all the intelligence of the universe, compressing billions of years of knowledge into every second of life.

"Don't you realize," Merlin said to his pupil, "that the history of the universe has brought us here to this second? We are the privileged children of creation, for whom all of this was made."

If your true source is in the subtle, unseen world rather than in the physical, then your body isn't really made up of cells. These are not the building blocks of life, nor are the atoms and molecules that cells can be broken down into. The body is built on invisible abstractions called information and energy—both of which are contained in your DNA.

But the wizard delves even deeper into the unseen world, knowing that your deepest beliefs are the most powerful creative forces. Your physical body grew out of the surging impulse of life contained in DNA. Without this impulse, information and energy are inert. Likewise your thoughts and emotions flow into the world from the unseen impulses of intelligence that make up your subtlest body, the causal body.

According to the wizards, the reason we all go to sleep at night is so that we can put all these bodies in order after the exertions of being awake and active.

But the subtlest work of all is done in pure silence. The next time you notice a passing moment of quietness when you have no thoughts or desires or feelings, do not take it as absentmind-edness. Your awareness has slipped between the cracks of the physical, emotional, mental, and causal bodies. In deep silence we return to the ultimate cause, pure Being. There you come face-to-face with the womb of creation, the source of all that was, is, or will be, which is simply yourself.

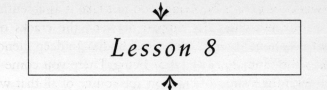

Lesson 8

Power is a double-edged sword. Ego power seeks to control and dominate. The wizard's power is the power of love.

The seat of power is the inner self.

The ego follows us like a dark shadow. Its power is intoxicating and addicting but ultimately destructive.

The eternal clash of power ends in unity.

Just before he left Merlin's care, Arthur became very moody. He was nearly fifteen, and he had rarely seen other people. "Are you sad about going out among *them*?" Merlin asked. "After all, you are of their kind."

Arthur looked away. "I am sad, but that's not the reason why."

"Then what is it?"

"I want to ask you something, but I don't know how, or if I should."

"Go ahead."

Arthur looked doubtful. "It's not about any lesson you've taught me. Yet more than anything I want to know—that is, if you would tell me . . ." He paused, tongue-tied.

"You want to know what it is like to be in love, perhaps?"

Arthur nodded, happy to have been saved by Merlin's intuition. The old wizard thought for a moment and said, "First of all, do not be ashamed, because you've asked about a truly important thing. There is something about being in love that cannot be captured in words, but come with me."

Merlin led Arthur out into a clearing where the noon sun shone. In Merlin's hand a lighted candle appeared, which he held up against the sun. "Can you see whether it is lit or not?" he asked.

"No," said Arthur. The sun was so bright that it made the candle flame invisible.

"But look," Merlin said. He held a ball of cotton next to the candle, and it was promptly burned up.

"What does that have to do with love?" the boy asked. But Merlin didn't reply. He only took a wild gentian flower and squeezed two drops of its juice onto Arthur's fingers. "Taste," he ordered.

Arthur made a face. "It's very bitter."

Merlin led him to a lake and told him to wash his hands. "Now taste the water," he ordered. "Is any trace of bitterness there?"

"No," Arthur admitted. "But what does this have to do with love?" Again Merlin didn't reply but led the boy deeper into the forest. "Sit still," he said softly. Arthur did as he was told. After a moment a mouse crept out into the field some yards away. A shadow passed overhead, but before the mouse could move, it was snatched up by an eagle, which flew off with its prey to a nest high in the cliffs.

Baffled, Arthur said, "But you said you were going to teach me about love. What did anything you showed me have to do with that?"

"Listen," his master said. "Like the candle that becomes invisible held next to the sun, your ego will dissolve in the overwhelming force of love. Like the bitter taste that is undetectable once it is diluted by the lake, your life's bitterness will be as sweet as the freshest waters when mixed with love. And like the prey devoured by the eagle, your self-importance will become a glint in the eye of the love that eats you up."

UNDERSTANDING THE LESSON

The power of love is the power of purity. The word *love* is used in many ways, but it is a sacred word to the wizard, because his meaning for *love* is "that which dissolves all impurities, leaving only the true and the real." "As long as you have fear, you cannot really love," Merlin cautioned. "As long as you have anger, you cannot truly love. As long as you have selfish ego, you cannot truly love."

"Then how can I ever love at all?" asked Arthur, knowing that fear, anger, and selfishness were things he experienced quite often.

"Ah, that is the mystery," replied Merlin. "However impure you are, love will still seek you out and work on you until you can love."

Love seeks out impurity in order to burn it away. There is no such thing as a loveless person—there are only people who cannot feel the force of love. Being invisible and ever-present, love is more than an emotion or a feeling; it is more than pleasure or even ecstasy. As seen by the wizards, love is the air we breathe, it is the circulation in every cell. From its universal source love permeates everything. It is the ultimate power, because without using force, love brings everything to it. Even in suffering, love's power continues its work, far out of sight of the ego and mind. Compared with love all other forms of power are feeble.

"Are you as powerful as a king?" Arthur asked Merlin.

"Why do you think a king has any power at all?" asked Merlin in reply. "A king's power is given to him by his subjects, who can revolt at any moment and take it back. That is why all kings live in fear—they know that everything they possess is actually borrowed. The poorest subject in the land is richer than a king—that is, until he gives away his power and bows down to it."

The real power in life is internal. To be able to see the world in the light of love, which can only come from within, is to live without fear, in unshakable peace.

There are many secrets to love that escape people's attention. To get love, you must first give it. To make sure that another person loves you unconditionally, you must place no conditions upon him or her. To learn to love another, you must first love yourself. So much of this seems obvious. Why, then, don't we act on it?

The wizard's answer is that love needs to be uncovered, stripped of layers of anger, fear, and selfishness that obscure it like old shellac. To achieve a totally loving life, purify the life you have. There is no right or wrong way to approach love. "A person desperately searching for love," Merlin said, "reminds me of a fish desperately searching for water." Life can seem extremely unloving, but it is really the eye of the perceiver, not the world "out there," that deprives anyone of love.

The first step to achieve love as a complete, unshakable aspect of your life is to redefine what you call love at this moment. Most of us think of love as an attraction to someone else, as a nurturing force that makes us feel cared for, as pleasure and delight, or as a powerful feeling or emotion. Although love is an aspect of all these definitions, the wizard would say that they are partial at best.

"All love as you mortals define it must fade and perish," Merlin said. "Your so-called love comes and goes. It transfers from one object of desire to the next. It quickly turns to hate if your desires are thwarted. Real love cannot change, it has nothing to do with an object, and it cannot become another emotion because it isn't an emotion to begin with."

Discard all false or superficial types of love and what is left? The answer begins to emerge with self-acceptance. Being an inner force, love is first seen inside yourself directed toward yourself. "Mortals go around in a fever, restless and anxious with love," Merlin said. "If they can't have their beloved, they think they will die. But love can't make you restless, not real love, because it never seeks to go outside. The most desirable beloved is just an extension of yourself. The love you think you will get from another exposes a limitation in your own awareness. To a wizard, all forms of love come from the self."

"That sounds incredibly selfish," Arthur objected.

"You're confusing the self with the ego, when in reality the self is spirit," Merlin replied. "Selfishness comes from the ego, which always wants to possess, control, and dominate. When the ego says, 'I love you because you are mine,' it is making a statement about domination or possession, not about love. Those who have truly learned to love have first stripped away selfishness. Then an entirely different experience begins."

"And what is that like?" asked Arthur. "Will I ever know it?"

"One day, after you have gotten over this restless fever, you will see a small light in your heart. At first it will be the size of a spark, then a candle flame, finally a raging bonfire. Then you will wake up, and the flame will devour the sun, moon, and stars. At that moment there will be nothing but love in the cosmos, yet all of it will still be inside your own heart."

LIVING WITH THE LESSON

Learning to set the ego aside happens in stages—there are many layers of isolation, fear, habit, selfishness, and anger that prevent us from experiencing love as the wizard knows it. The lead role in learning to contact the universal force of love can first be taken by your mind. The mind can take on a new perspective, then the reeducation of emotions and beliefs can follow.

What is the basis of the mind's new viewpoint? Simply that there is a force of love present everywhere, that it can be trusted to bring your own life into order and peace. Try the following exercise: go outside at night and consider the sky spread out with stars. For centuries humankind has looked at this scene and considered its incredible structure and beauty. As a map of nature's orderliness, this is a perfect example—looking at the night sky, we can appreciate the flow of time over billions of years that has nurtured every small step in the life of the universe, from the organization of the first hydrogen atom through the formation of stars to the advent of DNA. No thread has been dropped in that immense time span; every piece of information and energy has evolved in such a way to make it possible for you, the observer, to look into a cosmos that is the living picture of your entire past.

The forces in the universe are immense, beyond the grasp of the mind, yet the process that gave birth to hydrogen atoms, stars, and DNA was extremely delicate. Things could have taken very different directions, in fact an infinity of directions, that would not have resulted in what you recognize as yourself. What allows this balancing act to take place is organization and intelligence. As the wizard sees it, order cannot simply spring from randomness; it is innate in creation. Thus the titanic forces swirling through the cosmos do not war with one another; they are allowed to exist and evolve as part of nature's tendency toward growth.

Now take all these qualities together: order, balance, evolution, and intelligence. What you have is a description of love. It is not the popular ideal, it is the wizard's love—the force that upholds life and nurtures it. This is where the mind begins to realize that the force of love is actually real. In modern life we have grown used to randomness, to the notion that life is precarious and threatened at every turn. But the history of life shows that it has survived for billions of years; in fact it seems to create conditions for its own survival by means of some deep intelligence that is never threatened. No matter how hostile the conditions, life is inextinguishable.

You can apply this insight to your own life. Imagine its very beginning, when against billions of odds a single sperm managed to fertilize an ovum in your mother's womb. Your present identity depends entirely on that act. The chances against this single occurrence would make it seem impossible, but it happened effortlessly. Likewise, there have been millions of assaults against you from the environment, from pollution, radiation, even from random mutations within your cells; any one of these could have ended your chances of survival at any time from conception to the present day. Yet the intelligence and organizing power inside you has overcome these obstacles with effortless ease, despite all the struggle your conscious mind may think is necessary to keep life going. In truth, your conscious mind could not anticipate or plan how to conceive life, keep it going, or defend it from such terrible dangers.

Now, if this effortless ease can operate at the unconscious and cellular level, why not on the conscious? Can you see yourself riding the crest of the wave of life? In fact, that is what you are doing at every moment. Your personal impulses to think, feel, and act are like the crest of a wave, constantly falling forward into the future, yet constantly renewed from below—the surge of love that constantly upholds life is like the surge of the ocean that renews each wave.

Seeing this is the beginning of trust. If titanic forces like gravity and the immense energies that fuel stars manage to coexist without destroying one another, then your own life will be upheld. Fear and doubt say this can't be true; our deep belief in struggle is based on the notion that if we didn't fight to survive, we would be crushed by nature's random indifference. The wizard opens a different way, inviting us to step into a world where fear, violence, and destruction are reflections of our own mistaken beliefs. In the light of trust, as it develops slowly over time, you will find that you are a privileged child of the universe, entirely safe, entirely supported, entirely loved.

Lesson 9

The wizard lives in a state of knowingness. This knowingness orchestrates its own fulfillment.

The field of awareness organizes itself around our intentions.

Knowledge and intention are forces. What you intend changes the field in your favor.

Intentions compressed into words enfold magical power.

The wizard does not try to solve the mystery of life. He is here to live it.

It took a long time for the boy Arthur to fully appreciate that he had been trained by a wizard. Merlin had taken him into the forest a few hours after he was born, and not until he went back into the world years later did Arthur understand the curiosity caused by his association with a *wizard*.

"If you've really met Merlin," people would say (those who bothered to think the boy wasn't just crazy), "what spells did he teach you?"

"Spells?" Arthur asked.

"Charms, incantations, special words that give Merlin his powers," they said, thinking that Arthur must be either very dim or very deluded.

"Merlin did teach me about words," Arthur said slowly, pondering the question. "He said that words have power, that they cover secrets like trapdoors covering underground passages."

This explanation had a fine ring, but people still weren't satisfied. They wanted to know how Merlin's spells actually worked. "Well," Arthur replied, "when I was an infant, I remember Merlin saying, 'Eat.' When I was a little older, he said, 'Walk,' and if I stayed up too late he said, 'Sleep.' As far as I can tell I've been eating, walking, and sleeping ever since, so those must have been potent spells, don't you agree?"

No one did. They went away wondering if this doltish lad Sir Ector had taken in would ever amount to anything.

UNDERSTANDING THE LESSON

The power of words lies not in their surface meaning but in qualities hidden from view. Every word, for example, enfolds both knowledge and intent. Both of these are magical qualities. The magic of knowledge is that many layers of experience—in fact, an entire history—can be packaged in a few syllables. "Call your kingdom Camelot," Merlin advised the boy before he set off into the world.

"Why?" Arthur asked.

"It is a new word that does not have to bear the weight of history the way *England* does," replied Merlin. "People will identify it with you and everyone you gather around you. It will serve as a touchstone. The instant people say it, your entire reign and all your exploits will be opened to them, as if by touching a lever and opening the door to a cabinet of riches." Which turned out to be true.

All the richest words in the language open hidden passages of meaning and knowledge. But the second quality of words, intention, is even more powerful. Intent was being expressed when Merlin, like any other parent, told his child to eat, walk, and sleep. It is through these words that we all learned important functions, yet now that we know them, the words are not needed. You don't tell yourself to eat or walk or sleep anymore. The intention of the word has been absorbed into you, and now all you need is a reminder ("I guess I'll go to sleep now"), and the desired result occurs.

Is it really accurate to call this a spell, as Arthur did? Yes, because once a word's intention is absorbed, a spell has been cast in the form of a mental imprint. Say the word *school* to anyone, and immediately the experience of going to school will be triggered. Associations of success and praise will appear for a good student, of failure and criticism for a poor one. Our whole lifetimes are packaged inside us as imprints triggered by words. "Mortals are wrapped in words the way a spider wraps flies in gossamer," Merlin claimed. "Only in this case you are both spider and fly, because you imprison yourself in your own web."

It's certainly true that we all use our own words to imprint the habits that make life go on unconsciously. The business of identifying with names and labels has already been mentioned; these, of course, are all words. But which words will allow us to break out of old habits and limited identification? If every word lays down an imprint in the mind, is every word bound to be limiting?

"The paradox of words," Merlin said, "is that you have to use them to discipline and train yourself. Walking, talking, reading— all these are functions a baby lacks. It is up to mother and father to educate a child into the ways of the world, and that is done with words.

"The problem is that words carry psychological meanings too. It is through words that parents make children feel good or bad, right or wrong. The most powerful expressions anyone can use are *yes* and *no*. The effect of these two syllables is to build boundaries or break them down. Everything you think you can do has a yes buried somewhere inside it, usually uttered by a parent or teacher in the distant past. Everything you think you cannot do has a no buried in it, from the same sources."

"Why is that a paradox?" Arthur asked.

"Because although words tell us who we are, we are still more than they can tell. No matter how powerful the spell words cast, people can change. The power of words can create something new, not just a limit."

The wizard uses words to say yes to things that we have been taught to say no to. On one level, that is what this book is doing —weaving a new world of meanings to replace the old meanings we have all grown up with. But there is a deeper mystery here. Words enfold both knowledge and intention; therefore, framing an intention in words is the first step in making it come true. Two good examples are prayer and affirmation. Affirming things such as "I am good" or praying to God with words such as "Let me be healed" is more than just expressing thoughts verbally.

Whenever a word is backed up by intention, it enters the field of awareness as a message or a request. The universe is being put on notice that you have a certain desire. Nothing more is required to make desires come true than this, because the computing ability of universal awareness is infinite. All messages are heard and acted upon.

"Mortals and wizards are not so different as you may think," Merlin said. "Both are sending their desires into the field expecting an answer, but in the case of mortals, the messages are garbled and confused; in the case of wizards, they are crystal clear. No intention is ever ignored, but there can be obstacles to their fulfillment because so many conflicts are hidden in them, all the conflicts within the human heart."

LIVING WITH THE LESSON

To live with this lesson means to acknowledge that your every intention leads to some result. A wizard is someone who knows precisely how to inject intentions into the field and wait for them to come true. The rest of us are not that conscious. We are also constantly sending intentions into the field, but we do this unconsciously. Our desires are random or repetitive or obsessive, all of which are wastes of energy.

"You mortals assume that you have to work to make your dreams come true," Merlin said. "When in fact most of the work you run around doing is *preventing* your dreams from coming true." From a wizard's viewpoint, the less effort expended, the better. In their teaching, wizards show their pupils how to think in a more orderly, conscious, efficient manner. To do that, you first have to eliminate habits of thinking that obstruct the universe's ability to carry out your desires.

Imagine that your mind is a radio transmitter, bombarding the field with messages. If you sit quietly and observe your mind, you will see that it is full of mixed signals. The things we want to accomplish we also have doubts about; the person we want to turn into is also someone we aren't quite sure about.

The mind is similarly full of pointless repetition. It has been estimated that 90 percent of the thoughts anyone thinks on any given day are the same as those of the day before. This is because we are all creatures of habit, worry, and obsession. Finally, the mind is full of unconscious static, tracking back to the very depths of infant memory. You may be paying attention only to your conscious, willed thoughts, but in the background your unconscious mind is churning with its unfulfilled hopes, its old fears and wishes—in short, all the things that didn't seem to come true in the past.

Intentions are simply desires, and desires are linked to what you need. Therefore all this activity of the mind that isn't being fulfilled consists of old *needs* that didn't get fulfilled. Thousands of times in the past you have thought "I want" or "I wish" or "I hope," but nothing seemed to happen, or else different things happened that were less desirable.

"I wish I could sweep out your brain," Merlin once grumbled when Arthur was acting in a particularly muddled way. "Your thinking should be a clear flow; instead it's a war."

"Why can't you sweep out my brain?" Arthur asked innocently.

"Because everyone and everything inside it is you." Merlin sighed. "You have turned into all those old, repetitive conflicts, and they will not disappear until you change."

The first step toward change is *recognition*. Recognize that you have had at least a few hopes and wishes come true. Unexpectedly, without your having to do anything, people have called on the phone just when you needed to talk to them, help has come from unseen quarters, prayers have been answered. All of this is happening in the field. When you have an intention and send it into the universal awareness, you are actually talking to yourself in another form. As the sender of a message, you are an individual living here in time and space. But you are also the receiver of the message, in your guise as a higher self presiding over your space-time identity. And even more than this, you are the medium of the message, pure awareness itself.

To see yourself truly you need to see yourself as having these three aspects: sender, receiver, and medium. There are many variations on the theme: you are the wish, the wisher, and the granter of wishes. You are the observer, the observed, and the process of observation. This threefold state is known as unity. So sending an intention into the field and getting a response back isn't something you have to work to achieve. In your unified nature, fulfilling intentions is *all* you do; it's your full-time occupation. There isn't a single thought you can have that doesn't send back some result.

The problem is that we all overlook results that are too subtle, that don't immediately fit our goals, that don't coincide with our ego judgments about what *should* happen. "You mortals live in a world of *should* and *what if*," Merlin said. "I live in a world of *what is.*"

When you learn to quiet the mind and purify it of all its long-held conflicts, the simple reality of how the universe works —the *what is*—will unfold. We will talk more about that in Part III of this book. For the moment, take a little time every day to notice the contents of your mind. This act of noticing, although very simple, is one of the most powerful steps to bringing about change. What you don't see you cannot change.

Your ego may not like admitting that you are filled with denial, conflict, mixed intentions, shame, guilt, and all the other

69

confusions that darken the mind and prevent it from seeing the reality of *what is*. In fact, the ego prides itself on its ability to hide these things from you, on the pretext that you will suffer pain if you look into your mistakes, faults, and sins.

The second step is to learn how to *fulfill your intentions*. The steps are completely natural, but they have to be learned. Get the ego, with all its expectations and anticipations, to step aside. Instead of feeling you have to control the outcome of your intention, be assured that the field will do the work for you. Release your intention into the field of the timeless; the more expanded your awareness, the clearer will be the signal you are sending.

Finally, *be easy and natural* with the whole process. When all these steps come together, your intention will enter the field of awareness, which acts like a matrix to connect your individual thought with all that is. The effortless flow toward an outcome will not be impeded or obstructed by anxieties and attachments of the fearful ego.

In truth, none of the mind's darkness is sin. "Always remember," Merlin cautioned the boy Arthur, "God does not judge, only the mind does." Having all your heartfelt wishes come true is what God wants for each person; it is our natural state as creators of our own reality.

Lesson 10

*We all have a shadow self that is a part
of our total reality.*

*The shadow is not here to hurt you but to point out
where you are incomplete.*

*When the shadow is embraced, it can be healed. When it
is healed, it turns into love.*

*When you can live with all your opposite qualities,
you will be living your total self as the wizard.*

"You never seem to feel lonely," Arthur remarked to Merlin. There
was a wistful tone in his voice. The wizard eyed him closely.

"No, it's impossible to be lonely."

"Perhaps for you, but—"The boy stopped short, biting his lip.
But his feelings got the better of him, and he burst out, "It's quite
possible to be lonely. There's no one here in these woods except
you and me, and even though I love you like a father, still there
are moments . . ." Not knowing what else to say, Arthur stopped.

"It's impossible to be lonely," Merlin repeated more firmly.
Curiosity gained the upper hand over Arthur's other feelings. "I
don't see why," he said.

"Well, there are only two classes of beings you and I need
worry about in this matter," began Merlin. "Wizards and mortals.
It is impossible for mortals to be lonely because you have so many
personalities fighting inside you. It is impossible for wizards to be
lonely because they have no personality inside them at all."

"I don't understand. Who is inside me except myself?"

"First you must ask who this thing called myself is. Despite
the feeling of being a unique person, you are actually a composite

71

of many people, and your many personalities do not always get along—far from it. You are divided into dozens of factions, each fighting to occupy your body."

"Is that true of everyone?" the boy asked.

"Oh yes. Until you find your way to freedom, you will be held hostage by the conflict among your inner personalities. In my experience, mortals are always conducting inner wars involving every possible faction."

"Yet I still feel like one person," Arthur protested.

"I can't help that," replied Merlin. "Your sense of being one person is born of habit. You could just as easily see yourself the way I have described. My way is more true, because it explains why mortals seem so fragmented and conflicted to a wizard. All in all, it is so bewildering to meet a mortal that I often believe I am talking to a whole village inside one package of flesh and bones."

The boy looked thoughtful. "Then why is it that I feel so lonely? For to tell you the truth, Master, I do."

Merlin gave his disciple a penetrating look. "It does seem a wonder with all those people fighting to occupy your body that you could ever be lonely. But I have concluded that loneliness exists as long as other people exist. As long as there is 'I' and 'you,' there will be a feeling of separation, and where there is separation there must be isolation. What is loneliness but another name for isolation?"

"But there will always be other people in the world," protested Arthur.

"Are you so certain of that?" replied Merlin. "There will always be people—that is undeniable—but will they always be *other* people? Wait until you come to the end of the wizard's way, then tell me how you feel."

UNDERSTANDING THE LESSON

When you look closely inside yourself, you will find there are many personalities competing for the use of your body. For example, the conflict between good and evil gives rise to two personalities called saint and sinner. These never quit arguing, the one side forever hoping to be good enough to satisfy God, the other forever feeling "bad" impulses that cannot always be restrained.

Then there are the roles you identify with—child, parent, brother, sister, male, female, not to mention the work you do: doctor, lawyer, priest, child care provider, and so forth. Each of these has staked a claim inside you, shouting over the rest in order to put a narrow viewpoint forward. We haven't even touched on your sense of nationality and religious identity—these alone cause endless trouble.

These personalities are usually in conflict. What we call happiness is a state in which much of this conflict has died down. When you were born you didn't have this war going on, because babies are not conflicted about their desires. There aren't voices of good and voices of evil, for example, until the baby is old enough to learn these concepts from its parents.

"You can't become a wizard until you think like a baby again," Merlin said.

"How does a baby think?" asked Arthur.

"By feeling, primarily. A baby feels when it is hungry or sleepy. When sensations are presented to it, a baby can feel whether they are bringing pleasure or pain, and it responds accordingly. A baby isn't inhibited about wanting pleasure and avoiding pain."

"I don't see anything special about that," Arthur said. "Babies just cry and smile and feed and sleep."

"Many mortals would be lucky to do those things after they grow up," Merlin muttered. "Being here in this world in a state of contentment is a real achievement."

A newborn baby's innocent instinct about what feels good or bad is quickly lost. Voices begin to appear inside, at first the voice of mother saying "yes" and "no," "good baby" and "bad baby." When yes, no, good, and bad are in line with what the baby wants, no harm is done. But inevitably a conflict arises between the baby's needs and what its parents expect. The inner and outer worlds begin to clash. Very soon the seeds of guilt and shame are planted; the fearless temperament of a newborn becomes stained with fear. The baby has learned to doubt its own instincts. The inner impulse of "This is what I want" turns into a question: "Is it all right if I want this?"

We spend our whole lives working back to the state of self-acceptance we were naturally born with. For years the questions multiply, and into the secret caverns and dark cellars of the psyche we shove as much doubt, shame, guilt, and fear as we can. These feelings remain alive, however deep we hide them. All the inner conflicts that we find so hard to reconcile lead back to a shadow self.

"It's interesting here at court," Merlin once remarked to Arthur after he became king. "I didn't realize you mortals all held the same job."

"Do we?" asked Arthur. "What might that be?"

"Jail keeper," replied Merlin, refusing to say another word on the matter.

In a wizard's eyes we are all jail keepers of our shadow selves. The unconscious mind is the prison where unwanted energies are locked up, not because they have to be but because we have been so imprinted by years of yes and no, good and bad. Having pondered Merlin's words about being a jail keeper, Arthur went to him and said, "I don't want to be this way. How can I change?"

"Nothing easier," replied Merlin. "Simply see that you are playing both roles, jailer and jailed. If you are both sides of the coin, then neither must be you, for they cancel each other out. Recognize this and be free."

"I don't know how," Arthur protested. "How can I find this shadow self you speak of?"

"Just listen. Like all prisoners, he is tapping messages on the wall of his cell."

The shadow self is just another role or identity we carry

around, but it isn't one we show in public. Most of the time the shadow self is too embarrassed or fearful to be presented to the light of day. But there is no doubt that it exists, for each of us has invented our own shadow, a persona whose task is to carry all the energies we haven't been able to discharge. For a newborn baby the problem of holding on to "bad" or unhealthy feelings doesn't exist. The instant you throw something negative into a baby's environment, it will cry or turn away.

This is an extremely healthy reaction, because by expressing itself so freely, a baby can discharge energies that would otherwise cling to it. As we grew up, however, we learned that it isn't always appropriate to indulge in spontaneous expression. In the name of politeness and tact, or knowing our place, or doing what our parents said, each of us learned to hold on to negative energies. We became batteries with longer and longer shelf lives, until now as adults we hold on to anger, resentment, frustration, and fear that are years old. Worst of all, we have forgotten the instinct for discharging our batteries.

"You will be very interested one day to see how much you resemble a bomb," Merlin said to the boy Arthur.

"What's a bomb?"

"If you lived backward in time, which is the only sensible way to live, you'd know." Merlin thought for a second. "Imagine a pig bladder that you blow up until it bursts. A bomb works on the same principle, except that it bursts so hard that it kills people."

"My God, couldn't that be prevented in the future?" asked Arthur, alarmed.

"No, you don't understand. Bombs blow up *because* they kill people. That's the point. I only mention this because bombs are so much like mortals themselves, who go around ready to burst all the time. The explosion of shrapnel—that's what they're going to call the exploding bits—is nothing more than the explosion of rage made manifest. Indeed, if humans could explode and kill people without fear of reprisal, most of them would."

75

Ending the war inside yourself means bringing the conflict among all your personalities to an end. You can relieve the shadow self of its burden of held energies from the past and thus create a condition for inner peace, since it is fear of being hurt that makes your inner voices mistrust one another. But you can't begin to resolve these inner tensions until you know what your inner personalities are made of.

Personalities are always made of the same thing—some old energy attached to a memory. For example, let's say you remember being punished as a child for something you didn't do. The energy of resentment or injustice will attach itself to that memory, and you will start building a fragment of personality—a resentful child—that will live out its narrow view of things until that energy is released. The resentful inner child is just a memory waiting to discharge its held energy, and until that discharge takes place it will be stuck.

Because you have memories with happy as well as painful associations, inner personalities come in pleasant and unpleasant forms. It is pleasant to remember being rewarded for good work; it is unpleasant to remember being criticized. But these opposing memories don't cancel each other out; they retain their integrity and conflict with their opposites. It's in the nature of judgments to say "I'm right," even if the next experience is totally contradictory. The criticism or unfair punishment will be carried around, repeating its scenario over and over, while in the next compartment another energy of being fairly treated and well rewarded will be expressing its viewpoint.

You can easily contact these held energies. Sit for a moment by yourself in a quiet room. Breathe easily in and out. Now, without changing your breath, just notice its easy rhythm and flow. Don't go any further until your breathing is nice and settled. When it is, try to recall an extremely unpleasant incident from your past, one involving strong negative emotions, such as shame, humiliation, or guilt. Let's say you were caught cheating on a test or stealing. It doesn't matter whether the incident was petty or serious—what you're after is a lingering emotion.

Bring a vivid picture of this incident to mind and allow yourself to experience the feelings that went along with it. Now notice your breathing—it will no longer be easy. Depending on the kind of emotion you were recalling, your breath will have turned ragged or shallow; you might even find yourself gasping or holding your breath. These changes reflect the fact that the breath is a faithful mirror of the thinking process, and particularly of any remembered emotion. What you are experiencing are the three components we have been talking about: memory, energy, and attachment. When all three come together, you get the beginnings of a subpersonality.

All subpersonalities want the same thing: to express themselves through you. The crying infant, the lonely child, the frustrated adolescent, the hopeful lover, the ambitious worker—all these want to have a life through you. And so they do, after a fashion. No single personality ever finds complete fulfillment; therefore all must clamor to get their moment in the sun—or in the shadows.

The resulting conflict is what makes human life so ambiguous, so full of light and shadow together. The wizard, however, lives only in light. Like an infant, a wizard doesn't hold on to energy. Having released all those remembered attachments that fuel our inner warfare, a wizard has gone beyond personality to dwell in pure awareness. The way to move from the mortal state to the wizard's state may seem mysterious, but in fact it is completely natural. All that is required is *balance,* which the flow of life is perfectly capable of preserving.

There are many ways of releasing old energies. One of the most powerful is simply to acknowledge that they are there. Instead of denying that you feel shame or blame, for example, look at yourself and just say, "This is how I feel." Often this moment of self-awareness is enough, because ultimately all held energies are being trapped inside through denial. Overcome denial and half the battle is won. Acknowledgment is a form of self-acceptance. You don't have to say, "It's okay to feel shame and blame," because in fact these are energies you want to let go of, not perpetuate. But it certainly is okay to say, "I have these feelings. They are real."

One of the most effective techniques for overcoming denial is, once again, to use the breath. Lie down in a quiet room and let yourself relax. Now take in a breath any way you like, shallow or deep, fast or slow, then release it naturally. Don't use any rhythm or effort, just let the breath go. You might find yourself sighing or gasping somewhat; that's all right.

Now take in another breath and again simply let it go, neither forcing it out nor holding on. While continuing to breathe this way, let any available emotions or images float up to be released. This process can be aided by focusing your attention on your heart or any part of the body where you feel sensations—certain physical locations are closely associated with emotions.

As you continue this exercise, your held energies will start to flow outward. Symptoms of this discharge may include faint memories, shadows of feelings, or even powerful expressions of emotion, such as crying. (If your feelings get too powerful, just stop the exercise and rest with your eyes closed for five minutes.) Most people have so much stored energy that they quickly fall asleep doing this kind of breathing—that is a sign of deeply held fatigue being released by your body.

If you don't feel any release of energy in the forms I've just described, you are using your mind to hold on. The mind can be bypassed by changing your breath slightly: try panting shallowly and fairly fast. This rapid, shallow, rhythmic breathing will distract the conscious mind and allow energies to slip past it. You can do this kind of panting for a minute or two but no longer, as the release can easily become too powerful.

This exercise can be repeated to breathe out old held energies, but it is also very useful in learning to discharge any new emotion or feeling that wants to come out. Like any other aspect of yourself, your shadow wants to express itself and become free, and the first step is to find a natural, comfortable way to release negative energies rather than store them in hidden dungeons of the mind.

Lesson 11

*The wizard is the teacher of alchemy.
Alchemy is transformation.*

Through alchemy you begin the quest for perfection.

*You are the world. When you transform yourself, the
world you live in will also be transformed.*

*The goals of the quest—heroism, hope, grace,
and love—are the inheritance of the timeless.*

*To summon a wizard's help, you must be strong in
truth, not stubborn in judgment.*

After the boy Arthur left Merlin's woods, he lived with old Sir
Ector and his son Kay. He was given the position of squire, but
this was in name only. Arthur had no family or possessions. He
couldn't afford to buy his own clothes, and no one really
believed he came from a noble family. Behind Sir Ector's back
the stable boys used to throw mud at him, and the maids whispered that Arthur knew black magic.

As a result Arthur spent much of his time alone. One day he
was sitting on the edge of a grove of oaks staring at a battered
water pitcher made of lead when Kay happened to come across
him. "Did you steal that?" Kay asked suspiciously.

"No," Arthur replied, shaking his head. "I borrowed it."

"What for?"

"Alchemy."

Kay's eyes grew wide. He had heard that wizards had the
power to turn base metals to gold. "You were taught alchemy?" he

asked. Arthur nodded. "If you can change lead to gold," Kay said excitedly, "our family will be the richest in England. Show me."

Arthur nodded and gestured to Kay to sit beside him on the grass. Without another word he began to stare at the lead pitcher. After a moment Kay noticed that Arthur's eyes were closed. He waited impatiently, but when Arthur opened his eyes fifteen minutes later, the pitcher was unchanged.

"I think you're a fraud," Kay said hotly. "That pitcher's still made of lead."

Arthur looked unruffled. "Well, of course it is. It's just a reminder. *I'm* the one who's trying to turn to gold."

UNDERSTANDING THE LESSON

Alchemy is the art of transformation. As taught by the wizards, the secrets of alchemy exist to transform mortals from a state of suffering and ignorance to a state of enlightenment and bliss. Merlin said, "Alchemy is going on all the time. You can't stop transformations from occurring at every level of life. It's *your* transformation I'm interested in. Compared with that, turning base metals to gold is trivial." Alchemy is a quest, and the quest is always for the same thing—perfection. Just as gold is the most perfect of metals because it cannot be corrupted, perfection in a human being means freedom from pain, suffering, doubt, and fear.

"But what if human beings can't be perfected? What if we are truly as weak and imperfect as we look?" Arthur asked.

"The secret is not in *how* you look," replied Merlin, "but in how *deep* you are willing to look."

Quests are personal journeys, and every step is taken alone. But Merlin had much to say to Arthur before he undertook his quest. "I have told you often that this lump of flesh and bones is not your body, that this limited personality you experience is not your self. Your body is actually infinite and one with the universe. Your spirit encompasses all spirits and has no limit in time or space. The work of alchemy will unfold these truths before you."

When Merlin spoke these words, the age of wizards was almost gone, giving way to the new age, which would be ruled by reason. Reason holds that alchemy is impossible, and as wizards receded into the twilight of legend, people began to accept that they were in fact limited to living as finite packages of flesh and blood in thin wedges of time and space.

Because we take for granted that solid things are real, we assign reality to the solid stuff we are made of. The same atoms of hydrogen, nitrogen, oxygen, and carbon make up clouds, trees, flowers, animals, and your own body, but these atoms are constantly shifting and changing—fewer than 1 percent of the atoms present in your body last year are present today. Even in material terms it makes little sense to say you are solid stuff when underlying that solidity is a world of empty space and constant flux. The quest that is alchemy begins beneath the surface of atoms and molecules, behind the appearance of change.

Even as a boy Arthur was eager for his first quest, and he dearly hoped Merlin would provide him with a horse and a map. But Merlin said, "Maps are useless where you're going, because the territory ahead is constantly shifting. You might as well try to map flowing water."

Once you accept that you are the flow of life and nothing less, the quest for perfection becomes a quest beyond the boundless. The things that are perfect inside you are essence, being, and love. These cannot be bounded in time and space. When you walk across the room, does your love for your family walk across the room? When you get wet in the bathtub, does your essence get wet? Boundaries can be mapped, and the visible aspect of a human being can be charted as bone, muscle, tissues, and cells. The brain can be mapped as pathways for the incessant interactions of 10 billion neurons. Yet in both these cases the map isn't the territory. The essence, being, and love that make up a human being have a life of their own that begins and ends with the same invisible awareness.

"I can see you as a cloud of energies," Merlin told Arthur.

"And you can see me as the same, but even these are not the real you. They are just more stuff, only at a subtler level."

"What sorts of energies?" the boy asked.

"Let's call them light and shadow, playing around your form as you think and feel. The light is different when you are happy or sad, inspired or tired, excited or bored. Some mortals walk through this world as bright lights, others as somber shadows. But no matter how bright the light may be, it isn't as real as the pure silence inside you."

"Why don't I see myself the way you do?" asked Arthur.

"Because these energies serve as cloaks. Some are dense, some light, and no two people are layered in exactly the same way. Even so, all of you look like walking clouds. Until you peel away the layers around your soul, you will never realize the clear, timeless core that lies at your center."

LIVING WITH THE LESSON

In the lore of alchemy, the four elements—earth, air, water, and fire—mysteriously combined to arrive at a magical end product called life. It is undeniable that you are made of earth, air, and water that have been reshuffled from some earlier form, such as food. The fire that sparks these lifeless materials into life can't be distilled, however, because it isn't a visible fire, or even metabolic heat. It is the fire of transformation, pure and simple. Therefore you are the transformation, the transformer, and the transformed. You are your own alchemist, constantly transmuting dull, lifeless molecules into the living embodiment of yourself. This is the most creative and most magical act you will ever undertake.

There is no limit to the marvels of this alchemy. In any given moment you can be reading a book, digesting a meal, manufacturing proteins and enzymes, storing information as memory, growing, breathing, sensing your environment, healing a wound, replacing dead cells, warding off viruses, and countless other activities besides. All these transformations go on largely unnoticed. The alchemist is invisible, working behind the scenes, and few of us ever think to find out who she is. Her home isn't in time and space but in the timeless, beyond memory.

Sit for a moment and imagine that you can see your life as a scroll that unfolds as you examine events further and further in the past. Start unfolding this scroll until you see a familiar scene, such as the day you got your present job. See this clearly, and then go back a bit further, say to college, and go on unrolling the scroll through high school, grade school, kindergarten. See as clearly as you can the scenes when you were a young child, a toddler, and an infant. It doesn't matter if vivid images don't emerge; if you just have a feeling for what it was like to be yourself at those ages, that is good enough.

Now go backward to the day you were born—this will be pure imagination—then see yourself as a fetus, then as a collection of transparent cells formed into a ball. Watch the ball shrink until you are two cells, then one. Finally, cross over and imagine yourself before that, without even a single cell to attach yourself to.

As you cross this threshold, notice that your identity does not disappear. Even with no image to look at and no body, you remain what you really are—a viewing awareness that stays the same even though the scenery of your life constantly changes. This is your identity as awareness, a lively, wise alchemist who stands unattached, behind the constant show of transformation.

Now try to imagine this awareness disappearing. In other words, imagine a time before you ever existed. It cannot be done, because the alchemist isn't limited to the realm of time, where all events have a beginning and an ending. Likewise, you may scroll forward into the future and try to imagine yourself dead and completely gone. Again it cannot be done. When you reach the end of memory, feeling, emotion, imagination, and ideas, what still remains is yourself in pure form as a life impulse, ever flowing through the mirage of creation. That flow takes place as constant transformation, the alchemy of existence extending into and beyond all worlds.

Wisdom is alive and therefore always unpredictable.

Order is another face of chaos,
chaos is another face of order.

The uncertainty you feel inside is the doorway to wisdom.

Insecurity will always be with the quester—
he continues to stumble but never falls.

Human order is made of rules. The wizard's order
has no rules—it flows with the nature of life.

Small details of nature would often catch Merlin's eye, and in them he could see lessons. One day when he and Arthur were walking in the woods, they heard a jaybird scolding them from a nearby pine tree.

"Stop and look," Merlin said quietly.

The jay was a nervous, erratic bird. After chattering at the two intruders, it flew to another branch for a better view, then after a few seconds grew dissatisfied and flew to a third. Next it apparently forgot that they were there and hopped to the ground to investigate a pinecone. In a matter of seconds it splashed in a small pool, chased away a gray wren, and started pecking at a piece of rotten bark.

"What do you think of that as a way of life?" asked Merlin.

"Very little," replied Arthur. "He acts like a brainless feath-erball with no idea what to do next."

"So it appears whenever a creature lives solely trusting in God," Merlin said. "It spends its days following one careless impulse after another with no thought to the future, and yet it gets along well enough, you have to admit."

UNDERSTANDING THE LESSON

The nature of life is to contain both chaos and order. Patterns emerge from disorder and melt back into it. Your body is totally chaotic at certain levels—swirling atoms of oxygen enter your bloodstream with every breath, teeming enzymes and proteins fill each cell, even the firing of neurons in your brain is an electrical storm that never ceases. Yet this chaos is just one face of order, for there is no doubt that our cells are masterpieces of organized function, that your brain activity results in coherent thoughts.

Indeed, chaos and order exist so closely one to the other that they cannot really be separated. "You must first be chaos before you can be a dancing star," said Merlin. And that is literally true, for the swirling primordial gases that formed the early universe had to precede the birth of galaxies. Early on these gases exhibited no pattern at all, just the faintest tendency to be attracted to one another. Yet out of that faint hint of gravitational pull, a chain of events was set in motion that eventually led to the inception of human DNA, a molecule so complex that to disturb any one of its 3 billion genetic units could make the difference between life and death.

On a personal scale, everyone struggles with order and disorder. Things have a tendency to fall apart; what was fresh and ripe eventually decays; what was young grows old and dies. "Death is an illusion," Merlin said, "but the struggle mortals put up in the face of death is very real. No mortal actually knows what death is, yet the impending event is so fearful that mortals fight against it with all their might, not realizing the tremendous disorder and chaos they are stirring up."

The wizard knows that life has always organized itself from

86

within. Those same faint tugs of gravity that created dancing stars out of chaos exist at every level of nature. A rose can be totally certain that it will grow into a rose, even though as a seedling it may look no different from a bean or a violet, and in seed form its only claim to uniqueness may lie in minuscule twists of its twin strands of DNA. We humans, however, are very worried about turning out right, so we spend countless hours of effort and struggle to try to assert our own uniqueness.

"What does it matter if birds live without thinking, or if a rose is always a rose?" Arthur asked. "They don't have minds, therefore they have no choice but to be what they are."

"True, you mortals have free will, but you have far too high an opinion of it," Merlin replied. "I live without choices and find it a much happier life."

"Without choices? But you make the same decisions I do," Arthur protested.

Merlin shrugged. "You are fooled by appearances. Look at your hand. There is no doubt that it belongs to you, yet you do not choose how its cells grow; you have no notion of what makes its nerves and muscles move; you don't consciously grow nails or mend a cut when your hand is wounded, do you?"

"True, I don't have to do any of those things."

"They are no longer choices for you, in other words," Merlin continued. "These functions have been given over to an involuntary side of your brain, which takes care of them automatically. In the same way all the things that you devote so much time to— thinking, deciding, feeling, choosing, judging—I have given over to the automatic side of my brain. Which is just another way of saying that I surrender them to God."

"Then what do you use your conscious mind for?" asked Arthur.

"To appreciate this world and the miracle of life. I am a witness to all that is, and as a spectacle, I can assure you, nothing is more surprising or beautiful or satisfying."

Modern life is so full of pressures pushing this way and that that most of us react by trying to impose order upon it. Our society of chaotic forces is thus a society of endless laws and regulations. This isn't surprising, because humans thrive on order and are frightened by disorder. Disorder is unpredictable and out of our control, therefore it makes us feel stressed out. Think of a time when disorder and unpredictability suddenly crept up in your life: missing an airplane flight, having your car break down by the side of the road, hearing that someone you love has lost a job.

Almost always these events work themselves out; there is no real harm done to your existence, just minor inconvenience. Yet your nervous system probably reacted very strongly, expressing fear and discomfort when your plans went awry. The ego's response to chaos is to fight against it and to impose even more control. The next time you flew you probably double-checked your departure time and left early. The next time you drove you took precautions against the same breakdown occurring again.

The problem is that all this struggle, worry, planning, and controlling runs against the grain of life. Life compresses chaos and orderliness together. You cannot have one without the other. If you want to be in the flow of life, you can't struggle against it at the same time. Therefore the quester after perfection accepts that he is always going to be uncertain, that she is always going to feel off-balance. "The role of the disciple," Merlin said, "is always to stumble but never to fall."

Despite the fact that your ego hates unpredictability, the truth is that you have benefited from it again and again. Think for a moment about the unexpected opportunities that have come your way, offers of help you never anticipated, sudden brainstorms and inspirations, impulsive decisions to move or talk to a stranger that opened new horizons. This is the natural way to live. "Your life is already organized within itself," Merlin said. "Life flows from life, the bud unfolds into the flower, the child ripens into the adult. Trust in each stage, celebrate it, and allow the next one to come to you effortlessly."

There is a simple exercise that will show you how truly marvelous it is to lead an unpredictable life. Sit for a moment and imagine that you can view your life as a video in your mind. Start the video with the events of today and let them roll forward the way you wish tomorrow will turn out, then the next day and the next. Imagine yourself growing older: see the future you would want if you could have anything you desired. Let your fantasy roam where it will, and end up with your own death. Make it a desirable death, painless and peaceful.

Once you've done this go back and see *an entirely different video*. Begin with the events of today, only have them turn out differently. This is only imagination at work, so you can give yourself a wild, catastrophic life, or a dramatic one, or a saintly one. Take the video up to your death scene. Now go back and start over again. The point of the exercise is that all of what you have visualized is true—your future consists of not one scenario but all possible ones. They branch out from the present moment like invisible threads of potential. Everyone's life is like this; only our false sense of control makes us believe that we can impose order on what in fact is totally unpredictable.

The ego must examine its fears and stop trying to control. That is one huge part of the quest you are on. If you can accept the flow of life and give in to it, you will be accepting what is real. Only when you accept what is real can you live with it in peace and happiness. The alternative is a struggle that will never end because it is a struggle with the unreal, with a mirage of life instead of life itself.

Lesson 13

*The reality you experience is a mirror image
of your expectations.*

*If you project the same images every day,
your reality will be the same every day.*

*When attention is perfect, it creates order and
clarity out of chaos and confusion.*

After he became king, Arthur shared his experiences in the crystal cave with only one person, his wife, Guinevere. It was years before Merlin reappeared, and Guinevere thought of him more or less the same way she would think of a unicorn or some other mythic beast. "If he is as wild as the dark Welsh mountains they say he was born in, I should tremble to meet him anyway," she once told Arthur.

"He isn't like that," Arthur replied. "He's not like anything you could expect or anticipate."

"My lord, I have met wizards in the French court, or those who went by that name," Guinevere said. "Are they not simply old men with long, white beards who act very wise, and shake their heads as if seeing things we can't, and claim to have powers no one ever quite witnesses?"

Arthur smiled. "Such wizards have come my way, but Merlin wasn't one of these. I once said to him, 'How are you and I any different? To me we are just two people lying by a stream under a tree waiting to catch a fish for supper.' He looked at me and shook his head. 'It's true that we are just two people lying here as you say, but for you this setting is the whole of your reality, whereas the stream, the tree, and everything around us is the smallest speck on the furthest horizon of my consciousness.' "

Guinevere asked, "If he really lived in such a world apart from ours, did Merlin ever say how to reach it?"

"Yes," said Arthur. "He insisted that my version of reality—the tree, the stream, the woods—was completely illusion, a private hallucination my mind forced on me, while his world was open to everyone, since it is entirely a world of light."

Guinevere was puzzled. "But you and I are both seeing this room around us, as does everyone else we know. I don't think this is just an illusion."

"Then let me show you something," Arthur said. He asked the queen to leave their chamber and promise not to return until the stroke of midnight. Guinevere did as she was told, and when she returned she found that the room was pitch black, all the tapers extinguished and the velvet curtains drawn. "Don't worry," a voice said. "I'm here."

"My lord, what do you want me to do?" Guinevere asked.

Arthur replied, "I want to find out how well you know this room. Walk toward me and describe what objects are around you, but don't touch anything." His wife thought this a very strange test, but she did as she was bidden.

"That is our bed, and over there the oak dowry chest I brought across the water. A tall candelabra of wrought Spanish iron stands there in the corner, and two tapestries hang on either side." Walking cautiously so as not to bump into things, Guinevere was able to describe every detail of the room, which in truth had been furnished down to the last pillow by herself.

"Now look," Arthur said. He lit a candle, then a second and a third. Gazing around, Guinevere was astonished to see that the room was entirely empty. "I don't understand," she murmured.

"Everything you described was an expectation of what this room contains, not what was really there. But expectation is powerful. Even without a light, you saw what you anticipated and reacted accordingly. Didn't the room feel the same to you?

Didn't you tread cautiously where you feared you might stumble into things?" Guinevere nodded. "Even in the light of day," Arthur said, "we walk around according to what we expect to see, hear, and touch. Every experience is based on continuity, which we nurture by remembering everything as it was the day before, the hour before, or the second before. Merlin told me that if I could see entirely without expectations, nothing I took for granted would be real. The world the wizard sees is the real world, after the light comes on. Ours is a shadow world we grope through in the dark."

UNDERSTANDING THE LESSON

The wizard has completely freed himself from the known. To him the only freedom lies in the unknown, because whatever is known is past and dead. "Do you know why I keep saying that your world is a prison?" Merlin asked. "Because whatever the mind can conceive of must be bounded. As soon as you put words around an experience or enclose it in thought or say 'I know,' something wonderful and invisible has flown away. Boundaries are cages; reality is a delicate bird trembling in your hand. Hold it too long, and it will die."

If it is true that the unknown is your ticket to freedom, it is also true that the ego is more comfortable with boundaries. Our minds generate the same images day after day. These images are a mirror of who you are, yet the ego takes them to be real. "Isn't it obvious that a tree is a tree, a wall a wall, a mountain a mountain?" the ego asks. But these are only real in one state of consciousness—the waking state. In a dream you might sit in a field and watch the clouds pass over a mountain. After waking up you would realize that the mountain, the clouds, and the field were just random firings of brain cells giving rise to fleeting images. There is no proof that being awake is any different. "Real" mountains and fields and clouds have no testable reality outside the images that fire in your brain.

Arthur was shocked when Merlin dismissed the visible world as an illusion. "But I can touch things around me and find them hard. If I bump my head against a rock, I get a bruise," he protested.

"Images aren't just visible," Merlin reminded him. "You can touch things in a dream too, and feel the full range of sensations."

"Then why do I distinguish between being awake and dreaming? Why does everyone call one reality and the other illusion?"

"Habit. If mortals took this knowledge from wizards, they would learn how to do everything while awake that they now do in dreams. Then the boundaries would begin to melt, and reality would beckon you out of your shadow prison."

We all experience the new and the unknown, but few of us see the unknown as a force that is beckoning us. The unknown contains clues to another reality. What are these clues? They change every moment, but if you look closely at any image the world presents to you, more of your own self will start peering back. The seeming randomness of events will begin to resolve into form and meaning, as if part of yourself is saying, "I'm here. Can you find me?" Chance meetings, unexpected coincidences, premonitions that come true, sudden fulfillment of wishes, flashes of unpredictable joy, a sense of deep knowingness, the dawn of trust—all of these are shapes reality can take as it coaxes us out of our self-made prisons. We don't have to listen to this beckoning whisper. The choice is entirely personal. A decision must be made, in the recesses of your heart, between the known, which is stale but familiar, and the unknown, which is fresh, a field of infinite possibilities.

LIVING WITH THE LESSON

Living with this lesson means going beyond the frontier of the known. If you could forget everything and anticipate nothing, you would automatically find yourself piercing the boundaries that shield you from the perception of a higher reality. That higher reality is enmeshed in the familiar one you see and move through every day; there is no distance separating the two. Yet they might as well be millions of miles apart.

Along with habit and inertia, fear has much to do with keeping reality the same as it always was. Try a version of the test Guinevere took. Stand in the middle of a familiar room in pitch black one night. Now walk through it, coming as close as you can to the objects in the room without bumping into them. You'll notice that it's very hard to walk through even the most familiar room without a sense of apprehension. Most of us deeply fear blindness because of the uncertainty it would bring; the heart races at the thought of falling down or knocking things over.

Yet what are you really proving except that the known cannot protect you from fear? As well as you know your room, the apprehension is still there, and it is the same with the daylight world, only there the fear is buried a little more deeply. Instead of just the dark making us fearful, we need something more: an accident, a break in routine, the sudden loss of security. No matter how comfortable you think you are in the world of known things, the potential for disaster is never far from your subconscious.

You can get a taste of the unknown with another simple experiment. Blindfold yourself and sit down in your kitchen. Now ask a friend to put three foods in front of you without telling you what they are. Taste them by having your friend put a spoonful or morsel in your mouth. You will quickly recognize what each food is, but you should also notice that, in the split second of uncertainty before recognition dawns, you will taste something new—an unexpected texture, a nuance of flavor, a faint aroma—that you had forgotten was there.

This is the power of uncertainty. As long as you are certain about things, you are living within boundaries. Yet things you think you are so certain of actually have new qualities to unfold.

94

"God made this world," Merlin said. "So it must be interesting enough to keep His attention. If you find things growing tired or stale or predictable, perhaps it is you who have lost the capacity to be interested." Opening the way to uncertainty is hard for the ego to accept, yet it is the only avenue into the wizard's world.

Lesson 14

✦

*Wizards do not grieve over loss, because the only
thing that can be lost is the unreal.*

Lose everything, and the real will still remain.

*In the rubble of devastation and disaster are
buried hidden treasures.*

When you look in the ashes, look well.

Like all children Arthur eventually noticed death. He was four
or five when Merlin found him crouched in the forest staring
at a small pile of gray feathers, the remains of what had once
been a sparrow. "What happened to it?" the boy asked.

"That depends," Merlin replied.

"On what?"

"On how you look at it. Most mortals call that a dead bird.
By 'dead' they mean that its life has been destroyed. Wiser mortals, however, look deeper. They see that death is just a rearrange-
ment. The stuff that the bird was made of is returning to earth to
blend with the elements that gave it birth."

The boy thought for a moment. "Why does seeing this make
me afraid?"

"Memory. Whether you know it or not, you have formed
ideas about death since infancy, and as these unfold you remember the fear and pain attached to those memories." The boy was
too young to understand all that Merlin said, and like most children he stopped asking the really deep questions. He was satisfied with Merlin's explanations until years later, when it dawned
on him that death could happen to himself and not just animals.

"I think," Arthur said when he was twelve, "that I am likely to grow more and more afraid of death."

Merlin nodded. "As you experience more of the world, your memories will come back more and more strongly. But there is something else. Mortals fear death because they are afraid of losing their possessions. If you see a dead animal, you cannot say what part of it has died. After its last breath, the body weighs the same; the cells are the same. Only the breath is missing, and whatever lies beyond the breath.

"But mortals have houses and things in them. They have families and cherished experiences. Losing these becomes a terrible fright. But I'll tell you a secret. Nothing dies at the moment of death. Death is a beginning, not an ending. When mortals fear it, they are only holding on to their memories. No one really knows what death is like. Take the wizard's view and welcome all losses, even the ultimate loss of death."

"I'll try," Arthur said dubiously, "but you are right. There are lots of things I don't want to lose."

"Just loosen your grasp a little, then, and remember: whatever you hold on to is already dead, because it is past. Die to every moment and you will discover the gate to unending life."

UNDERSTANDING THE LESSON

In a world of change there must be gain and loss. The ego judges gain to be good and loss to be bad, but nature doesn't make such distinctions. As long as there is creation, there must be destruction. "You mortals would like to abolish death," Merlin said, "not thinking how the world would pile up with people, animals, and plants. The forest would soon be smothered under its own life force, the seas would writhe with creatures fighting for space and air, and the delicate beauty of nature's balance would be no more."

The cycle of birth and death becomes a matter of fear and struggle only when it becomes personal. After a lifetime of fighting to prevent loss, the ego sees dying as the ultimate defeat. For most people fear of death is too overwhelming to face; it is a subject pushed down into the subconscious and denied in everyday life. Or the denial is intellectualized, making death a metaphysical mystery that can be pondered from a safe emotional distance.

The wizards say that death is unknowable for a different reason, because normal experience, and with it our normal way of knowing, stop at the moment of death. Normal experience is oriented toward what we can see, hear, touch, smell, and taste. To this are added thought and emotion. Dying means letting go of the senses, leaving behind the material world, and crossing over to a new kind of perception. "If you only knew it," Merlin said, "I am dead already."

"That doesn't seem possible," Arthur rejoined. "To me being alive means eating, drinking, sleeping, and having experiences. Aren't you doing that all the time, just like me?"

Merlin shook his head. "Why do you think life and death can't coexist? At the same time that I am doing all those things you mention, I am also in a state of knowingness, aware of myself simply as myself, never to be born, never to cease to exist. Discovering such a state is what death opens up. If you are fortunate to make the discovery early, before dropping your body, so much the better."

"You're very lucky that you don't have to fear death anymore," remarked Arthur.

"True, but then I made a decision most of you mortals would shun. I decided to pursue death and catch her in my arms like a lover, whereas you are forever running away from her, as if she was a demon. Death is very sensitive, and if you demonize her she will stay away and keep her secrets to herself. In truth, everything you fear about death is a projection from your own ignorance. You simply fear what you know nothing about."

LIVING WITH THE LESSON

Death is an ultimate event, but before it happens there are many minor losses along the way. If you take a moment to think about it, you can easily see the pattern of gain and loss that runs throughout your own life. While they are occurring, losses seem painful, and the ego inevitably reacts to loss by wanting to hold on. Yet moving from childhood to adolescence is a loss from one perspective and a gain from another; getting married represents the loss of single life and the gain of a partner. Gain and loss are two faces of the same thing. The only thing in life that brings an absolute gain is the gain of awareness, which is what the quest is all about.

"Does it ever occur to you that you can't lose anything," Merlin asked, "because you never had it in the first place? The only thing you've ever really had is yourself. This self may spend some time in a house or a job, it may spend time in the presence of certain things or with a certain amount of money, but in time all that will change. Then all you have is a memory, an image, a concept. These aren't real; they are figments of the mind. Thoughts are like guests; they check in and check out, while you are still there. Regard objects and possessions the same way. They come and they go. What remains is yourself."

Life is full of adversity, small or large. The ego has taken on the burden of guarding your life. It defends you from loss and disaster and fends off the concept of death for as long as it can. But the wizard welcomes any adversity, any loss, for the following reasons, which you can apply to your own life: everything in creation is made of energy. After it is created, any given energy form must maintain itself for a certain time. After a period of stability, the life force wants to bring something new onto the stage. In order to do that, old, outworn patterns must be dissolved.

This dissolution still takes place in the name of life, for there is nothing but life all around us. However, the ego gets attached to certain energy forms that it doesn't want to see dissolved. A lump of money, a house, a relationship, a government—in their own way all of these are energy forms that we try to protect against the flow of time. People fight to the death, as the saying goes, meaning that they will defend something until dissolution is the only alternative.

In truth, such struggles are not necessary. You can't fight to make a rose bloom. You can't struggle to make an embryo evolve into a baby—it just happens, following its own rhythms. Your ego easily accepts this fact about roses and babies, but not about money, houses, relationships, and other things it gets attached to. But the wizard sees the same universal laws governing all of life. The ego didn't struggle to get you into this world, after all.

The ego's struggle is a form of opposition to life, because it seeks to impose *artificial life*. "Nature takes things away for its own good reasons at its own good time," Merlin said. "If you want flowers out of season, you can embroider flowers that will last forever, but who could pretend that they are actually alive?"

Likewise, whenever you sense the need to control and struggle, to keep people, money, or things attached to you when they move away, you are opposing the universal force that keeps everything in balance. "You will have to acquire trust before you can surrender your control. Your conditioning leads to mistrust, because you mortals want so desperately to believe that you're immune to the cycles of nature," Merlin said in some amusement. "Even as your bodies are born, grow old, and die, you fantasize about leaving behind immortal buildings and statues, reputations, and coffers heaped with wealth. Do as you like, but if you wish to escape pain and death, first escape this delusion that you are beyond nature."

When you can begin to see the seeds of opportunity in the ashes of disaster, then trust is beginning to grow. This trust comes in stages. First, start to see that the ego's judgments about loss are false. "Pain isn't the truth," Merlin said. "It's what mortals go through to find the truth." Second, look for the other face of disaster or loss, the tiny seed of the new that wants to be born. "When you look into the ashes," Merlin advised, "look well." Third, replace blame and complaining with a calm, sure knowledge that you are protected in nature's plan—whatever you have lost is temporary and unreal. It was bound to go, not because nature is cruel and indifferent but because every step you take toward the real is precious. In this light you will begin to see that loss and gain are just a mask. Underneath is the steady light of the eternal, which shines through everything, weaving unity out of chaos.

Lesson 15

To the extent you know love, you become love.

Love is more than an emotion. It is a force of nature and therefore must contain truth.

When you say the word love, *you may catch the feeling, but the essence cannot be spoken.*

The purest love lies where it is least expected—in unattachment.

The purest knight to serve Arthur was Galahad, yet he had in common with the king that he was born out of wedlock. There was no stigma attached to the fact that Galahad was Lancelot's natural son, yet when the day came for him to become the champion of a lady at court, Arthur shook his head and frowned.

"I would not have you be the champion of any noble lady," Arthur declared. Galahad turned scarlet and stammered, "But, my lord, every knight must serve some lady out of the purity of his love."

"What do you know of love?" asked Arthur, his tone so direct that Galahad flushed twice as deeply. "If you are so eager to champion a lady, I will give you three to choose from." The king forthwith sent for Margaret, an old scrubwoman with gray hair and warts on her nose. "Would you serve her out of love, fair knight?" Arthur demanded.

Galahad was bewildered. "I don't understand, my lord," he murmured. Arthur gave him a keen look and sent the old woman away. "Bring in another," he commanded. This time a newborn baby girl was ushered in. "If you found Margaret too old and

102

ugly to serve, what about this lady? She is nobly born, and you must admit her beauty." It was certainly true that the baby was quite beautiful, but Galahad was even more confused. He shook his head.

"This love you speak of is a hard master," Arthur said. He sent a third time for a lady, and Arabelle, a lovely twelve-year-old girl, entered. Galahad looked at her and tried to control his anger. "My lord, she is just a young maiden and my half sister," he said.

"You asked for a lady to serve," Arthur said, "and I have been generous enough to present you with three. Now you must decide."

Galahad looked stunned. "Why do you mock me this way?" he asked.

Arthur raised a hand, and in a moment the great hall was cleared, leaving the two alone. "I am not mocking you," he said. "I am trying to show you something taught me by my master Merlin."

Galahad looked up to see a softened expression on the king's face. "My knights serve ladies out of love, they say," Arthur went on, "and, despite their vows to love chastely, more often than not they feel a passion for the ones they serve, do they not?" Galahad nodded.

"And the more passionately attached they are to the ladies, the more their zeal to serve them?" Arthur asked. The young knight nodded again. "Merlin taught me another way to love," Arthur said. "Consider the old woman, the baby, the young girl who is your sister. These are all manifestations of the feminine, and as those forms change, what you call love changes with them. When you say you are in love, what you're really saying is that an image you carry around inside has been satisfied.

"This is how attachment begins, with attachment to an image. You may claim to love a woman, but let her betray you with another man and your love will turn to hatred. Why? Because your inner image has been defiled, and since it was that image you loved all along, its betrayal makes you enraged."

"What can be done about this?" asked Galahad.

"Look beyond your emotions, which will always change, and ask what lies behind the image. Images are fantasies; fantasies exist to protect us from something we don't want to face. In this case it is emptiness. Lacking love for yourself, you form an image to cover over the void. That is why being shunned or betrayed in love causes such pain, because the gaping wound of your own need gets exposed."

"Love is considered so beautiful and exalted," Galahad mourned, "but you make it sound horrible."

Arthur smiled. "What usually passes for love can have horrible consequences, but that is not the end of the story. There is a secret to love. Merlin told me the secret many years ago, as I impart it to you: when you can love an old woman, a baby, and a young girl in the same way, you will be free to love beyond mere form. Then the essence of love, which is a universal force, will be unlocked inside you. You will be unattached, which is the silent summons that love must obey."

UNDERSTANDING THE LESSON

When a wizard speaks of love, what he refers to is almost the opposite of what we call love. To us, love is a highly personal feeling; to a wizard it is a universal force. Falling in love for us is a condition that eventually fades; a wizard doesn't fall in love because he is permanently in the flow of love itself. But the greatest difference has to do with attachment. Attachment arises whenever you say, "I love you because you're mine." This form of love is really an extension of the ego, which always thinks in terms of "I," "me," "mine."

"You mortals call it love when you feel completely attached to another person," Merlin said. "Your fantasy is either to possess someone completely or to be completely possessed. But wizards call it love when they feel no attachment, no possession."

"Isn't that simply indifference?" asked Arthur.

Merlin shook his head. "Indifference has no energy or life to it. A wizard's love is incredibly alive and flows with the energy of the cosmos. For that to happen you must be like an empty vessel. Mortals are so full of ego that there's room for nothing else. A wizard is completely empty; therefore the universe can fill him with love."

Merlin spoke gently, almost tenderly. "Falling in love is a wonderful opportunity for you," he said. "Normally you live safely behind the walls of your own ego. You like your safety there, your lack of vulnerability. Falling in love tears down the walls, at least temporarily. You are exposed and vulnerable, just as you feared, but the overwhelming emotion of love makes this an ecstatic condition rather than the painful one you expected. At its best, falling in love means sharing the unknown with another soul, being willing to step together into the wisdom of uncertainty."

Wizards do not see forms of love as higher or lower—that is the language of judgment, and wizards don't judge. "If your enemy walks past you and insults you," Merlin said, "that is an act of love. The impulse of love started in your enemy's heart, only to be turned to hatred when it passed through the screen of memory. Your past experiences cause the impulse of love to become warped or twisted as it rises to the surface, but make no mistake, any expression would be loving if you could meet it at its source."

"Is it possible to build a bridge from the kind of love mortals feel to the kind you feel?" Arthur asked.

"You don't have to build a bridge, for there is only one kind of love," replied Merlin. "Personal love that you feel for another is a concentrated form of universal love; universal love is an expanded form of personal love. You can experience both to the fullest if you allow yourself to be open."

LIVING WITH THE LESSON

To some extent we all fall in love with images. We carry these images around inside ourselves, waiting until we find a match for them in the external world. Usually we are searching for someone either to reflect our own self-images or to repair them. One kind of love seeks a mirror, the other wants to add a missing piece. In both cases there is an underlying sense of need. Feeling incomplete in yourself, you try to bolster your lack through someone else.

"If you want to feel love as God feels it, you must fill all your voids, for God can love only from the state of fullness," Merlin advised. To be a perfect lover would mean to have no secret weakness or wound you want someone else to fix for you. Searching out your own voids is the first step, filling them with Being or essence is the second. This process is usually called learning to love yourself, but we must be careful with that term. Too often it is synonymous with learning to love your self-image. In the wizard's eyes self-image is simply ego; it is denial papering over the void of lack.

The real process of learning to love yourself would be better termed learning to love your Self, meaning your spirit. If you honestly look at your past, which is now stored as thousands of memories inside, you will always find a mixed bag—some experiences may have aroused love of self or others, many did not. Memories of shame, guilt, rejection, hatred, resentment, and other unloving feelings cannot be converted to love. These images are what they are. Accept them and move to a higher sense of Self, which is unconnected with memory.

Memory can only lock you into a suffocating sense of your personal past. Beyond memory is the quiet experience of Being, simple awareness without content. This is the region of love, the region of yourself entered through meditation. Many kinds of meditation exist; their tradition in both East and West is guided by the principle that you have a core of Being or essence that can be entered. Access comes not by thinking or feeling. Rather, to meditate is to go directly to the silent region within.

You can get a sense of what it is like to go beyond images through the following exercise: imagine a beautiful woman or

106

handsome man in your mind's eye, someone who represents your ideal object of love. See the person as vividly as you can, then change her or his face, making it older and older, until the beauty is gone and what you behold is wizened and wrinkled. Is your feeling of love still as strong as when you started? Most of us find it extremely hard to have the same feelings for a wrinkled, old face as for a young, beautiful one. Can you call it love when a mere change of image causes such an alteration?

"Why does love change?" asked Arthur.

"Because the emotion of love always contains its opposite. The strongest love you feel masks a hatred equally strong," Merlin said. "The only difference is that the love is in blossom while the hatred is still a seed."

Or try this related exercise: think back to a time when someone you deeply loved hurt you. It might have been a moment of indifference or betrayal, or it might have been an act that revealed your beloved wasn't perfect but only human. If you are honest with yourself, you will remember how violently and suddenly love can turn into other feelings. The hatred, jealousy, hurt, or indifference that sprang up was always there in seed form, hidden from sight by the love you preferred to feel. Why did you prefer it? Besides sheer pleasure there is another reason: ego. The kind of love that is attached to another person is really about yourself, because what keeps it going isn't what is real in the beloved but something far more binding—your own need to possess.

When you think you possess someone else, what you're actually doing is finding a way to escape yourself, avoiding your denied fears and weaknesses. Instead of confronting yourself, you look in the mirror of love and see perfect fulfillment in the emotions you feel for your beloved. This is not criticism. As a wizard sees it, love really is a way to experience perfect fulfillment, but it can't happen through fantasy. The mirror of love is a divine way to go beyond ego, but only after you have gotten to the pure flow of Being that lies like a secret jewel inside every feeling of love.

"Remember," Merlin said, "love is not a mere feeling but a

universal force, and as such it must contain truth." If you are able to go this deep, you will find that every emotion turns out to be love in disguise. Jealousy and hatred seem to be opposites of love, but they can also be seen as distorted ways to return to love. The jealous person is seeking love but has a distorted way of going about it; the hating person may desperately want love but hates out of despair at ever getting it. Once you stop seeing love as a mere emotion, it makes sense that a universal force is drawing everyone toward it—this is the wizard's love. Thus we should honor every expression of love, however distorted. Though few people may be able to experience universal love at its fullest, all are walking the path toward it.

Lesson 16

*Beyond waking, dreaming, and sleeping,
there are infinite realms of consciousness.*

A wizard exists simultaneously in all times.

A wizard sees infinite versions of every event.

*The straight lines of time are actually threads
of a web extending to infinity.*

Merlin's robe was embroidered with moons and stars, and the
boy Arthur wondered why that was so. "Let me show you,"
Merlin offered. He took Arthur and sat him on a hilltop. "Now
tell me the farthest thing you can see."

"I see the forest extending for miles until it reaches the horizon. That's as far as I can see," said Arthur.

"And what is farther than that?" Merlin asked.

"The edge of the world, the sky, and the sun, I suppose,"
Arthur said.

"And beyond that?"

"The stars and then empty space, extending to infinity."

"And would that be true if I turned you around?" asked
Merlin. The boy nodded. "Very good," the wizard said. "Now
follow me." He led the boy to the stream where they often
napped in the afternoon. "Now what is the farthest thing you
can see?" Merlin asked.

"I can't see very far in deep woods like this, only to the last
bend of the stream down there." Arthur pointed about a hundred
yards off.

"But you know that the stream runs to the sea, and the sea to the horizon?" asked Merlin. Arthur agreed. "Then the horizon would give way to the edge of the world, the sky, the sun, the stars, and infinite empty space, just as before?" Merlin said.

"Yes," Arthur replied. Once more the wizard looked pleased and led his disciple into the crystal cave. "Now what is the farthest you can see?" he asked.

"It is dim, and all I can see are the walls of the cave," said Arthur, "but before you ask me, I will agree that outside this cave are the forest, the hills, the horizon, the sky, sun, stars, and empty space."

"Then mark well," Merlin said in a louder voice. "No matter where you go, the same infinity extends in all directions. You are thus the center of the universe no matter where you go."

"That seems like a trick," Arthur protested.

"No, the trick is played by your senses, which fool you into believing that you are localized. In truth, every point in the cosmos is the same point, a focus for infinity in all directions. There is no here or there, no near or far. As the wizard sees it, there is only everywhere and nowhere. Knowing this, you would wear moons and stars too. Without the illusion of your senses, you would realize that the moon and stars are right here beside you."

"When will I realize that?" the boy asked.

"In time. As the turmoil of your soul settles, you will see the heavens in your own being."

UNDERSTANDING THE LESSON

If we believe our senses, space and time are not mysterious. Standing on a hill, we can see that the earth ends at the horizon and the sun rises in the sky. Time ticks by in seconds and moves from past to future in a straight line. Yet to a wizard time and space are infinitely mysterious. A wizard believes in a present that is eternal, he sees that all events occur simultaneously, and every place is the same point surrounded by infinity.

"Ordinary space-time is a veil that you haven't penetrated

110

yet," Merlin said. "As long as you rely on your senses, you will remain on this side of the veil. Once you go beyond your senses, however, you will find yourself in realms and worlds you cannot imagine now. Each realm is a state of awareness, and discovering new worlds depends only on refining your awareness until it wakes up to these realities that hover so near. Right now both you and I can see infinity in all directions, only we make very different use of it."

To make use of infinity, you must retrain your mental conception of time and space, discarding the raw perception of the senses. You already know that the edge of the world isn't the horizon, that the sun doesn't really rise in the sky. The facts that replaced these mistaken beliefs may seem quite solid, but they are also open to change. A wizard sees time, for example, as a fragile collection of threads woven moment by moment. Every time you make a decision, you create a new event line extending from this moment; until you made the decision, that thread of time didn't exist.

In seeing time this way, as subjective and creative, the wizard can weave his own version of events into the web and thus alter past or future. "Can someone really change the past?" Arthur asked.

"Of course," replied Merlin. "You mortals are in the habit of believing that the past creates the present and the present the future. This is just an arbitrary point of view. Imagine for a moment your own version of a perfect future. See yourself in that future with everything you could wish for at this very moment fulfilled. Can you see yourself there?" Arthur nodded, because he had suddenly had a vision of Camelot in all its glory.

"Very good. Now take the memory of that future and bring it here into the present. Let it influence how you will behave from this moment on. If you imagined peace and contentment in the total absence of fear, live that now. Whenever competing impulses of anger or fear or lack come up from the past, discard those memories and act instead on your future memories. Shed the burden of the past, and let your vision of a realized future guide you. Do you see what has happened?"

"I'm not sure," replied Arthur.

"You're living backward in time, just as a wizard does. Living tomorrow's dream today is always open to you. Who says you must live only the past? By living forward in time, mortals are always weighed down by the burden of memory; they allow the past to create the present. The wizard chooses to let the future create the present—that is what living backward in time really means."

"And you have changed the past, then, by no longer letting it influence your actions in the present," said Arthur.

"Exactly. But that is hardly the end of it. The past can be changed much more profoundly. When you learn that time is being invented in your own consciousness, you will see that there is no past. There is only the eternal now, ever renewing itself. Now is the only time that really exists. The past is memory, the future is potential. This moment is the pivot for any possible future you can envision. So change the past completely by seeing it as unreal, a phantom of the mind."

Living backward in time isn't a fantasy, since you are already living some version of the future at this moment. In your consciousness you carry around models of how things work; these models allow you to project your expectations forward in time. You anticipate that your friends will remain friends, that you will continue to have a family and a job. At a deeper level, your social model tells you that the country and the government will remain much the same, and so forth. At the very deepest level, your model of reality assumes that gravity, light, and other natural forces will not alter.

Having a model of how things will continue to work is so important psychologically that we suffer when that model is threatened by any profound or unexpected change in our lives; by the same token, we also use projections to give us a more fulfilled life than we have right now. We all have wishes, dreams,

112

fears, and beliefs—these are projections of our internal models—giving us a second life, so to speak, based entirely on projection. In a wizard's eyes most people look like railroad trains with blazing lamps in the front running down a track. All they see is what lies in the view of their headlights, with no regard for the infinite expanse of possibilities on either side.

Think of the railroad track as time. Our narrow sense of time is directly tied to our narrow beliefs. A pessimist believes that nothing will turn out right, which provides a single-minded model for the future. An idealist believes that higher values will prevail, and that too is a model of the future. When the pessimist meets with good luck or the idealist with less than ideal results, both will prefer their models over reality. This is not to criticize the usefulness of models but to show that they are less than real. Instead of meeting the present moment head-on, we are all living backward in time, using our projected futures to guide us in our present actions. But unlike the wizard we don't do this consciously.

Instead of falling prey to your subconscious, which is constantly impelling you to embrace a future that is predictable, you can seize control of your talent for projection. Live the highest ideal now. See a future based on the belief that you are cared for in the universe, that you are growing toward higher consciousness, that love, truth, and self-acceptance are already yours. You do not have to achieve these states in order to live them now. Living them now is how you will achieve them.

LIVING WITH THE LESSON

As we've just seen, dismantling your old assumptions about time and space is all-important, because what you take to be "real" time and space are actually prejudices inherited from childhood. "I call it the web of time," Merlin explained, "because I see myself as a spider sitting at the center of all events, which stream out from me like gossamer threads. It takes every event to create the web, just as it takes every thread, yet I can choose to follow one at a time if I wish." The wizard finds it easy to shift from local time to universal time, from seeing things in terms of isolated events to seeing them as a whole.

How can you learn to see time as a whole instead of as a single straight line? In the story Merlin showed Arthur how to see himself as the spatial center of the universe no matter where he sat. The same can be done with time. Consider this moment, then go backward in time to yesterday, last year, a decade ago. Keep going until you reach your birth, then accelerate and see past centuries, prehistory, the beginning of the world. Take the time line to the birth of the earth, the birth of the sun, the birth of stars. As you dissolve the stars and go back to the primordial universe, you will arrive at the moment of the Big Bang. Now your imagination won't be able, probably, to come up with images of a further past, but still you won't have to stop. There is no real beginning of time, because for any moment you call a beginning, you can still ask the question, What came before that?

Likewise, if you begin in the present moment and move forward in time, you may run out of images after you imagine the end of the world, the end of the sun, the end of the galaxies. But there will never be an end to time, because you can still ask, "What happens after that?" In short, time is an eternity extending in both directions, no matter what moment you choose as your beginning. This tells you two things: you are the center of eternity, and all points in time are actually the same. This must be true if eternity is equal from any point in time. It has been said that time is nature's way of preventing us from experiencing everything all at once. You could also say that time is nature's way of letting us fulfill our desires one at a time, which is, after all, the most enjoyable way.

In fact, any moment is every other moment, and what creates the illusion of past, present, and future is just the focus of your attention. Your mind is the knife that cuts the continuum of space and time into neat slices of linear experience. When you can use this power consciously, you will be a wizard.

"Write the word *nowhere,*" Merlin told Arthur, "then rewrite it as *now here.* You have in a nutshell the truth about space and time. You originated in a continuum that has no beginning in time or space. Being infinite and eternal, you come from nowhere. Yet this infinite, eternal continuum has manifested as this moment. Your mind and senses have localized eternity into a point, which is now here. The relationship between *nowhere* and *now here* is the relationship between infinity and this moment that you are now living."

115

*Seekers are never lost, because spirit is
always beckoning to them.*

*Seekers are offered clues all the time from the world of
spirit. Ordinary people call these clues coincidences.*

*To a wizard there are no coincidences. Every event
exists to expose another layer of the soul.*

*Spirit wants to meet you. To accept its invitation,
you must be undefended.*

*When you seek, begin in your heart.
The cave of the heart is the home of truth.*

Merlin had the strange habit of seeming to enjoy the occasional mishaps that befell the boy Arthur. If Arthur came home to the cave with cuts and bruises from falling out of a tree, the wizard would murmur "Good" almost inaudibly. One time in a lightning storm an old, rotted sycamore was hit and almost fell on top of Arthur. "Well done," Merlin muttered.

As softly as these comments were uttered, the boy felt sorely wounded. He vowed to himself to conceal any small disasters from his master, but the next day he was chopping firewood near the cave when the ax slipped. In a split second the blade had sliced through Arthur's shoe, barely missing his toes. When he yelled in fright, Merlin came swiftly and gave the shoe a sharp appraisal.

"Better and better," Merlin said softly. Arthur couldn't contain himself.

116

"How can you be happy when I'm hurt?" he cried.

"Happy? What are you talking about?" Merlin seemed to be genuinely confused.

"You don't think I notice, but whenever something bad happens to me, you seem pleased."

Merlin screwed up his face. "You shouldn't eavesdrop on conversations not intended for your ears, especially if they are conversations between me and myself." This reply only had the effect of making the boy extremely dejected. He was on the verge of running away to escape Merlin's stonyheartedness when the wizard took him by the shoulder.

"You think you understand me, but you don't," he said. Then his voice grew softer. "I wasn't rejoicing at your misfortune. I was rejoicing at your escapes. If you only knew it, these accidents of yours could have been much worse."

"Do you mean that you saved me from danger?" Arthur asked in bewilderment. Merlin shook his head.

"You saved yourself, or at least you're learning to. There are no accidents, despite what you mortals believe. There is only cause and effect, and when the cause is far away in time, the effect returns after you have forgotten it. But be sure that everything that befalls you, good or bad, is the result of some action in the past." Because he was young and because he trusted in his teacher, Arthur did not resist this new notion. He pondered for a second.

"You're saying that these mishaps are like an echo. If I shouted yesterday and the echo waited until today to come back, I might have forgotten all about it."

"Exactly."

"Then how am I learning to prevent these delayed reactions, if I've already forgotten about them?" the boy asked.

"By being more alert. Actions return to us over and over from different directions. So many kinds of cause and effect are working all around us that one must be very alert to see them. Nothing is random in the universe. Your past actions are not returning to punish you but to catch your attention. They are like clues."

117

"Clues? To what?"

Merlin smiled. "It would spoil the clue if I told you. Enough to say that you are not who you think you are. You live in many layers of reality. One of these we shall call spirit. Imagine that you do not know yourself as spirit but that your spirit knows you. What would be more natural than that it should call to you? The clues that fall out of the sky are messages from spirit, but you must be alert to catch them."

"But all I did was cut off my shoe with an ax and nearly get hit by a falling tree. It was mere coincidence that I was standing under that tree to get out of the storm," the boy protested.

"So you say, and so mortals like to say all the time. But if you look, you will see that a disguised clue is present in every coincidence. It is up to you to interpret them. I will tell you this, however. If that tree had fallen on you or if you had injured yourself today, I would not have mourned. I would have said, 'Spirit is difficult to heed.' Since you are getting better and better at avoiding disaster, I can say instead, 'He is learning to listen.' "

UNDERSTANDING THE LESSON

Of all the worlds the wizard inhabits, the two that are furthest apart are those of matter and spirit. These are also the two poles of our existence. It is natural to swing from one pole to the other, to move from faith to skepticism, until the opposites are united. At the present moment the swing is away from the material pole, although that pole still dominates everyone's thinking. When we speak of cause and effect, we mean that material things interact—the sun pulls the earth around itself, striking a match creates a flame, lightning hits a tree and it falls. The fact that humans inhabit this arena of cause and effect makes no difference; the laws of nature operate without regard to us.

The wizard doesn't accept this materialistic viewpoint. To Merlin every action in nature, however insignificant, had a human meaning. This is because he looked to the opposite pole, the world of spirit, to find the place where cause and effect actually begins. "You mortals need to be much more vain," he told Arthur.

"More vain? You often say that nothing so crammed with vanity has ever been created," Arthur replied.

"That I still hold to be true, but if you were even more vain, you might see how unique you are. The universe is organized around your destiny and obeys your least whim, yet you go around complaining that God and nature are totally indifferent."

"If God isn't indifferent, then why doesn't He show His intentions?"

"Ah, you must search to find that out. Perhaps this whole world was intended as a game of divine hide-and-seek."

"Then it would be a very cruel game," Arthur said, shaking his head. "I would not feel kindly toward a loving father who refused to show his face to me. What would his so-called love amount to then?"

"Don't be so sure the decision was his," Merlin cautioned. "If God has seemed to depart, perhaps you sent Him away."

What Merlin touches on here is a matter of perspective. If you see the world as material, then events happen without regard for human existence. On the other hand, if you see that spirit is the primary force in the universe, then nature's seeming indifference may be a mask or contain a hidden message. Wizards see through the mask, finding a message from spirit in every event, but the messages remain disguised so long as our perception is clouded.

That is why Merlin called the messages *clues*. To have clues you must have a mystery. In this case the mystery is how the world manages to be both material and spiritual at the same time, how the same act can appear to be either the work of a totally indifferent God or the sign of His loving presence.

"I do not indulge in paradoxes just because I like to," Merlin said. "Perspective is everything. If someone runs at you with open arms, you can consider it an attack if you feel the person is an enemy, an embrace if he is a friend. A baby may kick and scream when its mother scrubs its face, but from the mother's perspective, it's a loving act to clean off the dirt.

"In the same way most of the events you call misfortunes or even divine punishment are really born of compassion, for God always takes the kindest way to correct imbalances in nature. It is you who build up these imbalances, which He must purify in order to save you from deeper misfortune."

Seekers are those who try to resolve the seeming paradox of God's indifference and God's love. They look into the crises that most people shun, because from hurt or failure or disaster one can seize the deepest truth. This enigma is worth devoting one's whole lifetime to solving. "Don't mistake me when I say that spirit leaves clues all around," Merlin said. "I don't mean that the clues are obvious or that the mystery will be easily cracked."

LIVING WITH THE LESSON

If spirit is showering clues all around you, how can they be spotted? First, you must be willing to see these clues. They crop up in many forms: meeting someone you just thought about, hearing a word that just flashed through your mind, having plans go awry only to find a hidden benefit, noticing that too many coincidences are occurring in your life to truly be coincidences. Spirit often begins to speak in these ways—they might be called first encounters. Narrow escapes, lucky accidents, and intuitions that come true fall into this category also; in all these cases the normal patterns of cause and effect are stretched, sometimes broken. If you try to apply the kind of logic that says A causes B, which causes C, the explanation will not work, because these coincidences are too far-fetched and too personal. The real question isn't Why did this happen? but Why did this happen to me?

Of course self-pity can generate the same question—Why did this happen to me? One must learn to ask it in a different way, out of curiosity freed from self-pity. The ego thinks that having something odd or bad happen can't possibly be good. Yet any occurrence is meant to be *useful*. Spirit sometimes has to use a higher kindness, teaching a hard lesson out of compassion so that truly disastrous things are averted. And what of the truly disastrous? These events the wizard sees as the best that spirit could do, given the complex web of cause and effect that each person is enmeshed in.

Yet often there is no obvious spiritual content to the clues of daily life. They are simply the first beckoning, a call to awaken. Everyone notices unusual events, but unless you see them as clues, you won't ask what they are about. You will simply let them happen and pass on by. They will remain meaningless.

It is important to have a framework of understanding, to know that another aspect of yourself—spirit—is shining through the disguise of the material world. If you are willing to accept that spirit could be beckoning to you, the clues will begin to change. Instead of being coincidences that quickly fade from your mind, clues will begin to take on spiritual overtones. In this category we might put having prayers answered, going through near-death experiences, seeing auras or divine light, and sensing the presence of angels. Our society is putting unprecedented attention on such things, but still they are often mistaken for "phenomena." A phenomenon is by definition impersonal. A wizard would say that these clues are actually highly personal; they are meant to guide someone.

You can't decipher the hidden meaning, however, until you ask for it to be revealed. "Don't expect spirit to write a book and read it to you," Merlin said. "Life is creative, and so is spirit. Each clue meant for you is tailored to your level of awareness. Be grateful that spirit remains out of sight, just around the next bend. Rejoice that you can be a seeker all your life, for if spirit delivered its secrets once and for all, you would be left with pleasant memories but a listless and dull future."

Because spirit is on the move, constantly creating your life from the invisible source of all life, you must be alert every moment to understand its ways. Sometimes clues hit like a bolt from the blue, sometimes they cross your path as silently as a cat stalking in the predawn light, sometimes they smile and deliver a shiver of bliss. The great joy of crossing into the wizard's world is that the whole world comes alive. Nothing is dead or inert anymore, because the least thing can serve as a clue to the great search for who you really are. "Respect your mystery. Nothing is more profound," Merlin said. "But pursue it ruthlessly, trying to rip the veil away at every second. This is what makes life rich, that it has more to offer with each clue it reveals."

Immortality can be lived in the midst of mortality.

Time and the timeless are not opposites. Because it embraces everything, the timeless has no opposite.

At the level of the ego, we struggle to solve our problems. Spirit sees that struggle is the problem.

The wizard is aware of the battle between ego and spirit, but he realizes that both are immortal and cannot die.

Every aspect of yourself is immortal, even the parts you judge most harshly.

When Arthur was a very young king, he heard reports of a madman who lived deep in Camelot forest. "Pay no attention to these idle rumors," he was told by wiser heads. "It is just some lunatic who has sealed himself up in a hut and will soon die."

But something in Arthur was stirred. He summoned his knights and set out to find the madman. After several hours the royal party came upon a clearing not far from the main road through the forest. In the middle of the clearing stood a hut made of mud and wattle, so poorly put together that bare branches stuck out everywhere. Arthur dismounted and walked up to it. There was no door, only a small window to let in air.

"Who is there?" he asked.

"One who is not of this world," a weak voice answered.

Arthur stood for a moment, thinking. "I would converse with you, whoever you are. Come out on order of the king."

"I have no king. Leave me alone," the voice said.

"But you have no food or water either. You need help," Arthur said.

"I don't need your help," the voice said, and then would not utter another word. His courtiers wanted Arthur to depart, embarrassed that he took interest in a lunatic, but instead the king gave orders that anyone who had information about the man should be brought to him. Several horsemen rode off into the forest, returning with a poor woman dressed in rags.

"This is the wife," one of the horsemen said, releasing the clearly confused and frightened woman.

"Please be calm. I only want to help your husband," Arthur said.

The woman still trembled but replied, "He doesn't call me wife anymore. My Will has sworn to stay walled up in that hut until he either dies or receives a sign from God."

"Why?" asked Arthur.

"Grief, my lord. We had a son he loved above anything in this world. My Will is a woodcutter, and one day he set off into the forest with our boy, who was six. Will was intent on his work, and when he wasn't looking the lad slipped away. We called and searched until we was frantic, then after a day the little body floated downstream. Our boy was drowned, and my husband cannot forgive himself."

The story greatly saddened Arthur. "Grief is no reason to kill oneself," he said.

"So says I," the poor woman declared. "But he has sworn that until God Himself comes to tell him why our son was taken away, he will curse this world and have nothing to do with it. 'I have watched the kind of suffering God permits all my life,' he says, 'and I won't have no more to do with it. If He won't appear to explain Himself, I'm as good as dead anyway.'"

Despite the poignancy of the woman's story, Arthur couldn't help but be intrigued by this man's curious approach to God. "Is this account true?" he asked into the hut. There was a low grunt, but otherwise Will the woodcutter had nothing to say.

"I am going to spend the night here and converse with this poor wretch," Arthur announced, sending the rest of the royal party home. The courtiers were reluctant to leave their king in the forest alone, but eventually he persuaded them to ride away and camp within half a league. Night fell quickly, and no moon rose. Arthur sat beside the hut wrapped in his cloak to ward off the damp.

"In some ways I feel closer to you than to anyone else in my kingdom," he began. "I am new to my rule, and I keenly feel the suffering that surrounds me. The poor, sick, and crippled exist everywhere, but their plight is mine also, so long as I am their king. I have spent many sleepless nights wondering how to solve the evils of this world. It seems that I could spend my whole life and fortune to combat the misfortune I see around me, yet like spring wheat the seeds of woe would sprout twice as thick next season."

"I am waiting for God," the voice inside the hut suddenly interjected. "I don't need to hear your speeches. Let Him answer for Himself."

"Fair enough," replied Arthur. "But let this be my business, that I see myself in you. I had a master named Merlin, and he told me that there is only one solution to evil, which is not to struggle against it but to realize that evil does not exist."

"Foolish words," the voice said. "Find another master."

"You need to listen more," Arthur insisted. "Merlin said that good and evil constantly clash in combat; they were both born thousands of lifetimes ago. And as long as there is light and shadow, good and evil will live on."

"In that case you should despair and shut yourself up in this hut with me, for you have seen God's true feelings toward this world. He wants us to suffer," the voice said bitterly.

"I felt as you do for a long time, but then Merlin showed me that there are two paths in life. On one path a person tries to win the reward of heaven, and if he lives virtuously, he will attain his goal. But even in paradise there are seeds of discontent, and eventually, out of boredom, or out of fear that heaven isn't deserved, a

125

person will start to move the other way. He will sink and eventually find himself in hell. Hell must exist if heaven does, but it is just as temporary, for in time a person will tire of its torments and start to rise again. Thus the first path a soul can choose is a constant round, moving from heaven to hell and back again."

"If what you say is true, we are mocked as well as damned," the voice said with deeper bitterness. "Who can love a father who holds out paradise only to send us back to hell?"

"You are right," Arthur said. "My master pointed out that very thing. But then he told me of a second path. The key to this path is the realization that heaven and hell are created by ourselves, that we are the ones who keep the cycle going. Because we believe in duality, there must be evil as the opposite of good, just as light must have shadow or it would not be light. Having seen this, we can make a different choice."

"Which is?"

"To renounce duality, to refuse both heaven and hell. Beyond the play of opposites, Merlin said, lies a timeless realm of pure light, pure Being, pure love. 'All this business of good and evil,' he said. 'Stop chasing your tail and walk away from it.' I cannot speak for you, my friend, but to me that is the divine message. If God is to appear to us, it is through our own understanding of what is possible. Our will is free, and we can chain ourselves to the cycle of pleasure and pain forever. But we are equally free to walk away and never suffer again."

Arthur stopped, suddenly feeling how strange it was to be talking this way to a poor wretch he had never met. "I'm sorry to intrude on your grief," he said, finally. "I will take my leave now." The man in the hut made no reply.

Arthur got up, pulled his cloak tighter, and moved off into the forest. He was a hundred feet away when he felt a glow at his back and the crackle of flames. Fearing that the madman had set the hut on fire, he turned and began to run back, only to stop in his tracks.

The hut had turned into a ball of brilliant white light, and

126

out of it stepped an angel, who said, "I was told by God that you mortals knew a secret, and as always He was right. You know that God isn't simply in heaven but far beyond, in the realm of pure spirit." And with these words, the angel vanished.

UNDERSTANDING THE LESSON

The essence of this lesson is explained in it, that there are two paths in life. The first path is the acceptance that duality is real, that the good and evil we confront every day are simply fact, and we must do our best to struggle against them. The second path is to see duality as our choice. Although everything in creation appears to have its opposite, one thing doesn't: wholeness. The totality of spirit has no opposite because it embraces everything. To choose the second path, you have to be willing to renounce your struggle against evil. This is the way of the wizard.

There is no doubt that when we see evil we react with fear and anger. From this reaction struggle is born, and because people want evil to go away, the struggle seems to be legitimate. But what if fear and anger are the cause of evil? What if our reactions keep breeding the same cycle, which never ends? With these questions the second way was born. It isn't that struggle is wrong, that we must submit to evil. But the end of evil is a serious matter, and wizards have stepped into the arena of discussion to propose that an end is possible, albeit not through the means we have used for so long.

LIVING WITH THE LESSON

You cannot renounce the duality of good and evil as long as that is what you experience. A deeper experience, one that is beyond words, must replace it. *Wholeness* and *spirit* are only words until they become real to you personally. *Reality* always means experience; therefore the question is how to experience the realm of light that Merlin spoke of. "Be patient with yourself. The fading away of duality takes time," Merlin said. "And then unity will be born automatically."

Because spirit is always beckoning, there are countless opportunities to come into contact with it. The first steps have already been marked out—be willing to follow the clues of spirit, meditate to find the pure silence within yourself, know that the goal of spirit is true and worth pursuing.

This lesson reinforces those steps, but it adds a new ingredient. As much as people complain about evil and struggle against it, evil has remained with us for countless ages. As a result one can become very discouraged, like the man sealed in the hut. But he is named Will for a reason—our free will is what allows us to break out of the cycle of good and evil. This is the promise held out in this lesson. The way of the wizard is compassionate, because it solves the problem of suffering as the light of spirit draws nearer.

*Wizards never condemn desire. It was by following
their desires that they became wizards.*

*Every desire is created by some past desire.
The chain of desire never ends. It is life itself.*

*Don't consider any desire useless or wrong—someday
each one will be fulfilled.*

*Desires are seeds waiting for their season to sprout.
From a single seed of desire, whole forests grow.*

*Cherish every wish in your heart, however trivial it may
seem. One day these trivial wishes will lead you to God.*

It was a miraculous Christmas Day when Arthur pulled the sword
from the stone. In all the tumultuous crowd that witnessed the
deed, none was more surprised than the young Arthur himself.
Where is Merlin? he thought, certain that the wizard had accom-
plished the feat with magic. But Merlin did not show his face.

Deep in the night, long after everyone had gone to bed,
Arthur still sat up, wondering if his destiny really was to be king.
"I need you, Master," he prayed. Suddenly there was a light
under the door. Arthur leapt to his feet and opened it, but the
wizard hadn't come. It was Kay, his adoptive brother.

"How are you faring?" Kay asked. Arthur did not know what
to say, but as he turned back into the room, he took a sharp
breath. "Hold your light higher," he said. Kay raised his candle,
and its light fell on three objects that had appeared on Arthur's
bed—a straw doll, a broken slingshot, and a cracked mirror.

"Do you see those?" Arthur asked in a strange voice. Kay looked confused. "I see them, but they mean nothing to me," he said.

"I wished for Merlin's help, and now these have appeared. This doll was my first toy," said Arthur, picking it up. "I must have been two when Merlin made it for me. This broken slingshot I made from deerskin and forked willow when I was eight. This cracked mirror I found in the woods when I was twelve. Do you know what they have in common?" Kay shook his head. "They were the most important things I ever owned, each in its own time, and now look at them."

"Worthless trash," Kay muttered.

"Yet I am overjoyed to see them, for now I know Merlin has guided me all along. You see, Kay, when I was two I only wanted toys; when I was eight I wanted only to hunt sparrows and squirrels; and when I was twelve I only wanted to look in a mirror to see if girls would find me ugly or handsome. All these things I have put behind me, yet each one was a stepping-stone to this very moment. One day so shall I put away the crown, although it is my sole wish and destiny today."

Kay was a simple, stout soul who revered the monarchy. He was shocked. "Why would anyone throw away the crown?" he asked in bewilderment.

"Because there will come a time when it is as trivial as a doll, as useless as a broken sling, and as vain as a mirror. I think that's what Merlin wanted me to see."

UNDERSTANDING THE LESSON

Desire holds a peculiar place in our hearts, because although each of us moves through life desiring one thing after another, our old desires get thrown away as if they never mattered. Desires never end, no matter how many wishes come true, and at the same time no single desire lasts long enough to allow us to put desire fully behind us.

"You are only human, and your nature is to want more and more," Merlin said. "Desire is what leads you through life until the time comes when you desire a higher life. So do not be ashamed that you want so much, but do not fool yourself into thinking that what you want today will be enough tomorrow."

It is obvious that desires never end, yet that has not stopped people, often very spiritual people, from trying to renounce desire. In the West, Christians condemn the weakness of the flesh because of its base desires; in the East, Buddhism blames desire for being at the root of the endless cycle of pleasure and pain. But in a wizard's eyes there is no reason to cast judgment against desire.

"When you go out into the world," Merlin told the boy Arthur, "you will seize a prize that all men want. This will turn thousands against you and lead you into years of strife to win your crown."

"Then I won't take the crown," Arthur said, much troubled.

"No, that is not the way," Merlin replied. "Desire leads mortals into all kinds of turmoil, but it is in God's plan for you to have desires."

"But desire blinds people and makes them selfish. It stirs up violence, as you just prophesied. It creates ignorance and sets one person against another."

"Those are all *uses* of desire," Merlin pointed out. "There is a mystery here, as always, that only the seeker will solve. Is desire good or evil or neither? I will give you a clue. To find out the true nature of desire, you must begin without judgment. Honor each and every desire you have. Cherish those desires in your heart. Do not struggle to get what you want; trust that your higher spirit has put the desire inside you, and leave it to spirit to make your wishes come true. You may find that the evil in desire is actually not desire itself but human struggle over it."

The wizard does not struggle to have his own way, to grab or win or possess, because he sees desire in a larger pattern laid down by spirit. "Seen for what it really is, desire expresses your

131

ultimate need to rejoin perfection. From the moment you were born there was never any hope that you would feel fulfilled by achievements or possessions or status. Nothing outward was ever going to work."

"Then why did God create so many objects of desire?" Arthur asked.

"Why not? What is wrong with wanting more of this world if it is worth wanting at all?" replied Merlin. "Look upon desire as the willingness to receive what God wants to give. This world is a gift; there was no compulsion for the Creator to make it. God's ability to grant unto you is limited only by your ability to receive."

"Perhaps so, but why didn't God simply provide a direct path to Himself?" Arthur asked.

"He did. Desire *is* the direct path, for there is no quicker way to God than your own wishes and needs. Why should God give you something before you want it? When you look at your own desires and judge against them, have you ever asked yourself why? To judge desire is to judge its source, which is yourself; to fear desire means that you fear yourself. The problem is not with desire but with what happens when your desires are blocked or frustrated. Then the struggle and judgment begin.

"If you could see a way to fulfill all your desires—which is what God has had in mind for you all along—you would see that without desire you couldn't grow. Imagine yourself as a child who never wanted to go beyond playing with toys; without new desires constantly arising inside you, you would be trapped in perpetual immaturity."

LIVING WITH THE LESSON

Merlin's speech on desire touches a nerve, because we live in a society where people are able to have more and more material things. The net result, however, has not been to make us perfectly happy. Quite often what lies behind affluence is a spiritual void.

This doesn't mean that wanting to have a house, a car, and a bank account is wrong or shameful. The spiritual void wasn't *created* by wanting material things. It was created by turning to externals and expecting them to do what they can't do. Externals can't fill spiritual needs. The saying that a rich man has as much chance to enter heaven as a camel does of passing through the eye of a needle isn't a condemnation of wealth. It simply points out that money has no spiritual value. Money isn't the gate to paradise.

The wizards have always taught that desire must be seen as a path. In the beginning desires are about things like pleasure or survival or power. But in time the path of desire leads beyond these gratifications. They are not baser desires but earlier ones. Just as a child outgrows toys at a certain age, the desire for more and more will eventually lead a person into a natural phase where the desire for God becomes all-important. "Don't worry about becoming a seeker after God," Merlin said. "You have been a seeker since birth, only at first the God you sought was toys, then approval, then sex or money or power.

"All of these you worshiped and wanted with great passion. Rejoice in them when they are the desires of the moment, but be prepared for them to fall away. The great problem you will face will be not desire but attachment, holding on when the flow of life wants you to let go."

The exercise for this lesson is a pure thought experiment. Sit and imagine the thing you want most passionately right now. Perhaps it is a certain car or a life of wealth or some kind of success in a relationship. Try to pick something you're still pursuing so that you can feel how powerful the pursuit of desire really is.

Now back up to a desire or wish in the past, one that has already come true. It might be your last new car or a successful project or a chunk of money. Compared with your current desire, this old one will feel different. You won't feel so keenly the hunger to pursue the old desire because you've already tasted its fulfillment. What you are experiencing in this contrast is how life pushes you forward. Yesterday's desire had its own impulse for fulfillment, which has now shifted to today's desire. This forward-moving impulse isn't random. It has carried you from an infant's wants to a child's to an adolescent's to an adult's.

The path of desire is incredibly powerful and never ends; only the objects of desire shift and change. What the wizard sees is that at their deepest level our desires contain the evolutionary impulse of life itself. To want to live isn't a mere survival instinct—it is a path that unfolds. Life does not like being blocked, which is why Merlin said that problems with desire only arise when some obstacle is put in its way. A healthy baby learns that whatever it wants is good when its mother is pleased to fulfill its needs.

If a positive model of desire is established early, then the baby will grow up with natural desires that match its true needs. A psychologically healthy person, in fact, can be defined as someone whose desires actually produce happiness. But if the baby is imprinted with the opposite notion, that its desires are shameful and are only grudgingly met, then desire won't develop in a healthy way. In later years the adult will keep searching for fulfillment in externals, needing more and more power, money, or sex to fill a void that was created in his or her sense of self as a baby; the person's very sense of being is judged to be wrong.

In extreme cases desire becomes so distorted that its need turns into a need to kill, steal, commit violence, and so forth. These desires can cause untold harm, both personally and socially. Yet no one knows, seeing a murderer or thief, where his or her values went astray. To a wizard all desires begin in the same place, at that point where life simply wants to express itself; it is the obstruction or condemnation of desire that creates the problem. Unhealthy expressions of desire simply reflect unhealthiness in a psyche that desperately needs to know itself, just as all of us do, but has—at least for the time being—failed.

Therefore it is vitally important to come to terms with the nature of your desire, to realize that in the divine plan all your desires are meant to come true. God isn't blocking you from having anything and everything you want. It is you who believe deep down that you don't deserve anything and everything. Such self-judgment creates blockages in the natural flow of life, but once they are removed the path of desire becomes a joy, because it is the shortest and most natural way to God. No desire is trivial, because every desire has a spiritual meaning. Each is a small step leading to the day when you desire the highest fulfillment, which is to know your own divine nature.

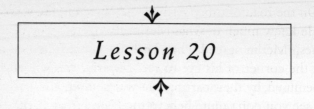

Lesson 20

The most good you can do for the world is to become a wizard.

It was the last day they would spend together. The boy Arthur stood by the side of the road that led out of the forest. Looking over his shoulder, he searched for Merlin's glade, but it was no longer there. A thick patch of woods had grown overnight, swallowing up the glade and with it the opening to the crystal cave. Arthur felt a pang, knowing that this loss would be felt by all mortals, not just himself.

"I won't be coming back, will I?" he asked. Merlin, who was standing by his side, shook his head.

"No need to. You are done with me."

I doubt that I'll ever be done with you, Arthur thought. It seemed that even after all his years of training, there was more left to ask his teacher than the day they began. Reading his mind, the wizard said, "I wanted to give you a parting gift, and I could think of nothing better than this." He pointed to the road beneath their feet, which had also appeared overnight. "Roads are the sign of the wizard. Or did you know that?"

"No."

"Then remember what I say. A wizard is one who teaches by walking away, and when you can walk away yourself, you will be a wizard. Although you may fancy that you own a part of this earth, in fact you only walk it. In spirit you are the dust on the road, the restlessness in the wind. You mortals build homes to protect yourselves from the world. To a wizard home is this moment, and moments are always moving—"

"On the road of time," Arthur said, finishing the sentence for him. He knew much of what Merlin had to teach by heart.

"Yes," Merlin agreed. They both fell silent. The boy glanced out of the corner of his eye to see if Merlin was saddened, or at least bemused, by their parting. He was neither.

"I see you don't quite believe me," Merlin said. "But walking away from me really is the greatest gift I can bestow upon you." And with that the boy's unwilling feet started to move. There was a bend in the road a hundred yards away, and every step Arthur took toward it seemed to change him a little. The years he had spent with Merlin began to fade into a dream, while his curiosity about the world increased.

By the time he reached the bend in the road, he couldn't wait to see what lay around it. All the action and desire of a world that he'd never known became something he had to be a part of; now his feet were flying in their eagerness to get out of the forest. The very image of Merlin faded from his mind, until only a lingering voice remained, saying, "I have led you into the secret places of your soul, now you must find them again, this time by yourself." In a moment this voice too faded away. The boy passed the bend, kicked up a puff of dust, and smiled. He suddenly knew that every time he saw a road he would think of Merlin.

UNDERSTANDING THE LESSON

Walking a road is a sign of detachment, and wizards teach that in detachment lies true freedom. A free person lives in spirit, just as a wizard does, and is able to do far more good than can ever be done outside spirit. This viewpoint isn't yet acceptable in society, because you and I and everyone we know have been conditioned to believe otherwise. We are attached to everything and believe that attachment is what makes our lives work.

Our sense of attachment begins with our relationship to this earth. Mortals, the wizards say, are under the illusion that they own the world or control its fate. As the wizards see it, the world has a spirit that oversees our welfare; we live sheltered within her spirit and are allowed to shape our own fate. But spirit can never be owned or controlled. "You want to have the whole world, don't you?" Merlin asked Arthur.

"No, I don't think so," replied the boy.

"Oh, you do, believe me. You mortals are like a spark that will one day set a whole field afire. The spark looks tiny, but it spreads and spreads."

"Do you mean that we will destroy the world?" asked Arthur.

"That depends. Spirit cannot be destroyed, and if you come to see yourself as spirit, you will join with the spirit of this earth. The alternative is to ignore spirit, and if you choose that way, you will have no regard for the earth. Her pain will seem remote to you."

Merlin pointed to a large rock. "Kick it," he said. Arthur did as he was told.

"Ow." He winced.

"Strange," commented Merlin. "The rock got kicked, but you're the one who cried out."

"What's strange about that?" grumbled Arthur, half suspecting that the wizard had made him kick the rock harder than he'd planned.

"This was a lesson about spirit. When you kicked the rock, it was yourself you hurt. The rock didn't protest, because the earth never does. She is secure in her spirit. Security in spirit is what the earth has to teach you mortals. But if you become enraged at your injury, which the rock merely gave back to you, you will be tempted to ignore spirit. You will want to crush the rock, destroy it, and turn it to your uses, all because the earth is kind enough not to cry out when you kick her."

It is in the nature of spirit not to protest. There is no harm you can really do to spirit, and although humans have inflicted appalling harm on the earth, the final result is always that we harm ourselves. We don't respect our own spirit. We regard our-

138

selves with fear and anger. "You have lost faith in faith," Merlin said. "You no longer seem to trust in trust." What this means is that the qualities of spirit, which include love, faith, and trust, must be known and experienced before they can do much good.

Most people struggle against their will; they resort to fear and anger because they feel that these paths have been forced on them. Willingness to live in peace depends on not being directed by these negative energies, and that can only happen by adopting the wizard's way. "If you want to do good for the world, be completely unselfish and become a wizard," Merlin said. "If you want to do good for yourself, be completely selfish and still become a wizard." This may sound like a paradox, but ultimately all spirit is spirit. You walk the earth as an individual, but you also walk it as part of the earth. Therefore, as you regain yourself, you regain the world.

LIVING WITH THE LESSON

The wizards do not discourage doing good. Detachment isn't the same as indifference. "When you see suffering, go and relieve it," Merlin said, "but make sure you don't come away with the suffering sticking to you." This advice aims right at the heart of compassion. The root of the word *compassion* is "to suffer with," and that is the way most of us interpret it. We assume that a compassionate person has taken on the suffering of another, but if that were true, then compassion would double the suffering of the world, not relieve it.

True compassion is not negative. One is able to feel another's pain but remain secure in spirit. The earth behaves toward us like that. Although the drama of human affairs is played out on the earth's stage, shedding our blood in her fields and building wealth on her shores, she is detached. The forests, fields, shores, and mountains don't rise and fall because of us.

If you don't accept that the earth has a spirit, this detachment becomes indifference. In the name of indifference, the earth is being despoiled. Compassion for the earth is only possible when you join your spirit to hers.

What does it take to join the earth's spirit? This book is an attempt to provide an answer. The wizard's way began in myth, in the deep memory of humanity, when we were still cradled in primordial forests. Merlin represented a nature spirit of great magic and power then. Today there are no nature spirits because mortals decided to separate themselves from nature. The old impulse to live inside nature gave way to its opposite, the impulse to conquer her.

This impulse has worked itself out to the point of near disaster. The return to nature is being desperately sought on all sides, perhaps at the last hour. The wizards never separated from nature, so they have nothing to return to. They wait to welcome us when we turn back to spirit. Their secrets reveal that, if you want to rejoin nature, the path is to regain your own nature, which is pure awareness. There is nothing "out there" except a mirror for what is "in here." If you want to go home again, realize that home is this present moment.

All the power and fulfillment humans yearn for exist in the present moment. In the now is tremendous energy, more than the mind can imagine. Nothing could be closer, yet nothing slips away faster. That is the mystery and the paradox. To solve it, realize that *you are this moment*. All the power that is present here must be found within. Everyone has some days full of energy, excitement, and optimism, and other days marked by fatigue, confusion, and pessimism. What makes the difference? Some people think the answer lies in bodily cycles, or the play of random forces, or fate, or luck. But the wizards say the answer lies in your ability to be present. When you are in the moment, you touch the source of life. Time itself flows from this moment and no other. Therefore, if you want to ride the crest of time, you need all the energy you can get, and that energy is found within the moment.

One can't help but wonder how the present moment ever

140

got away. You can answer this yourself with a simple exercise. Sit for a second and consider how memory works. When you see someone's face but can't quite remember his name, what do you do? If you struggle to remember, the very effort seems to shut down the power of recall. But we've all experienced how a forgotten name or fact will suddenly come to us when we're not trying to remember at all. Just letting go of the whole business seems to activate the power of recall.

Desire works the same way, although fewer people are aware of its mechanics. Because we all want things, it's easy to fall into the trap of constantly working, worrying, and struggling to get what we want. Yet the wizards say that if you let go, the mechanics of desire take care of themselves. This seems mysterious, but consider this: do you really know how lost memories return to you? Your conscious mind can't force you to remember things, yet the mind is quite capable of retrieving anything and everything it has ever known.

In much the same way, your conscious mind can't fathom how the universe makes desires come true. And just like the person struggling to recall a name but getting nowhere, people thrash wildly to fulfill their desires, never realizing that effort is the problem, not the solution. These points have already been covered in this book, but I'd like to reintroduce them at a deeper level. At this very moment you are a wizard. You are perfected in spirit; you have never separated from God or nature. All that has happened is that, in your struggle not to feel pain, you've started to block the present moment. Memory and desire veil the spirit. They do so because long ago you began to fear for your security here on this earth. Insecurity is the motive for attacking the earth, for if we trusted that we are nourished and upheld, none of us would be quite so hysterical about surviving.

"Trust in trust, have faith in faith," Merlin said. "That is the only solution when you have lost trust and faith." In the heart of ourselves, each of us is nothing but trust. Being and love are also innate parts of ourselves, but it is trust that allows us to breathe easy, to accept the earth's spirit as our own. And the technique for remembering this is as simple as the technique for remembering anything else. Allow yourself to stop believing that struggle is the answer. Appreciate in silence the life that is meeting you at every moment. With this silent acceptance comes the tremendous energy that is hidden in the present, and in that energy are abundance, peace, intelligence, and creativity. All these are the gifts of silence wrapped inside the spirit of the earth.

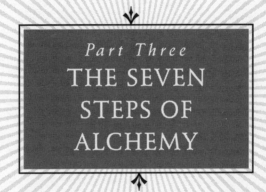

Part Three

THE SEVEN
STEPS OF
ALCHEMY

In King Arthur's time no quest elicited more passion than the search for the Holy Grail. Every one of Arthur's liege knights dreamed of acquiring this elusive prize, which would bring God's protection and blessing to their king. Knights doing penance in order to receive a vision of the Grail were a common sight, and painters competed to make each rendition of the Last Supper more splendid than the last.

"It is nearly impossible to convince mortals that quests are never for outward things, however holy," Merlin had once told Arthur. He remembered those words whenever Grail fever reached its pitch, which was usually in the long, dark months of winter, when the knights were bored and restless. The younger ones in particular were forever champing to quest to the Holy Land or to the castle at Monsalvat or to any place, mythical or real, where the Grail might be kept.

The king kept himself aloof from this fervor. "If you want to go . . ." he would say, his voice trailing off.

"What? Don't you believe in the Grail?" Sir Kay asked impetuously. Having once been considered the king's brother, before Arthur pulled the sword from the stone, Kay took liberties no one else dared.

"Believe? I suppose you would have to say that I do," Arthur replied quietly, "but not in the way you think, not in the way you yourself believe."

This answer was too subtle for Kay, who bit his lip to keep from asking a more insolent question.

"Is the Grail real, my lord?" Galahad said in a much milder tone.

"You ask as if you think I've beheld it," Arthur said.

"I don't know whether to believe that myself," Galahad replied haltingly, "but there are tales."

"What kind of tales?"

"Concerning Merlin. It is said that he himself brought the chalice from the Holy Land, where it had laid in secret for many centuries."

Arthur pondered this for a moment. "Like all tales, there is a grain of truth to that." The court stirred, for this was the first time the king had ever admitted any connection to the treasure they all dreamed about. But Arthur had nothing more to say.

One night in earliest spring, when the fields were thawing and jonquils no longer than a thumbnail had come into bloom among the fading Christmas roses, a fire could be seen at a great distance outside the walls of the castle. Around it sat Sir Percival and Sir Galahad, who had pledged to go on a holy retreat together. It was too early to take such a retreat deep in the woods, where the last snows of winter were still piled up in dirty drifts under the tree shadows, so the two knights prayed and fasted in a small tent within sight of the king's chambers.

"I once mistook my dream of capturing the Grail for an idle whim," Percival began. "Every knight wants to stand first among champions, but for years I have turned my back on my desire, thinking it a plaything of my pride. But I tell you, Galahad, my soul burns for this thing."

"The king says it isn't a thing," the younger knight reminded him.

"He also says Merlin brought it into England. You heard him yourself, didn't you?" Percival's voice rang with an edge of challenge, and Galahad merely nodded. Sometimes prayer and penance light more fires than they put out, he thought. Certainly Galahad had to admit that he shared Percival's growing desire.

"If anyone is fated to capture the Grail, surely it must be one of us," he said, throwing some dry hazel brush into the fire and watching it flare. "We are the only band of knights who truly live to protect the peace and not just to raid the countryside and spread terror. I don't know if my heart is pure enough to gain the

146

Grail—I'm not so vain or stupid as to believe it must fall into my hands—but my heart will be sore until I try."

At that moment the two men heard the crunch of footsteps breaking through the thin layer of ice still covering the ground nearby. They tensed, waiting for the stranger to identify himself, when a faintly mocking voice said, "Don't be frightened, and pray grant me safe leave. I need a fire, if you be kind enough to share one."

Percival looked at Galahad, then called into the darkness, "Be off and build your own. This is a retreat of two knights who must have no exchange with the world's impurities for a time." A mocking laugh came back in reply.

"Build my own fire, you say? Then I shall do just that." Before these words were fairly out, Percival jumped to his feet in alarm as the ground beneath him burst into flame. Galahad looked around in amazement to see that a circle of fire now surrounded them, sprung from the frozen earth itself. Before he could cry out, a tall figure, gaunt as an old fir, walked through the flames and stood over them.

"Merlin," Galahad said, controlling his emotions. "What brings you here after this long leave?"

"Not your insolent friend," Merlin replied, eyeing Percival, who was trying to maintain whatever shred of dignity a man can when his backside is on fire. "Sit down, sit down." The wizard beckoned. Percival felt the embarrassing pain vanish, and he took his seat next to Galahad, with Merlin opposite. Neither had ever set eyes upon him before, but Arthur's description had been accurate down to the wizard's crewel slippers of worn black moleskin.

"Don't stare," Merlin said. "I'm thinking."

"About what?" Percival asked.

"And don't interrupt" was all the wizard had to say in reply. After a moment his rather frosty expression softened. "Yes, I believe you are telling the truth. Now the only problem is what to do about it."

147

"The truth about the Grail?" asked Galahad. "We certainly do want to follow this quest." Merlin examined him approvingly. "You recognized who I was without foolish introductions, and now you come close to reading my mind. Very promising," Merlin said. In his natural modesty Galahad looked down at the ground, hoping that Percival would not begrudge him this unlooked-for scrap of praise.

"Your king spoke aright, you know," Merlin said. "The Grail isn't a thing you can run after on horseback like a fox. It isn't made of gold or jewels, and therefore it brings no one any benefit to hoard it in secret. And possessing it doesn't confer God's blessing, any more than not possessing it does."

Percival, who was growing more and more agitated, finally interrupted. "How can you say that? The Grail *must* confer God's blessing."

Merlin stopped him with a scathing look. "My dear clod, if all this world is God's creation, then how could any part of it, however remote or small or unimportant, be less blessed than any other?"

"But there is a Grail, isn't there?" asked Galahad. "The king told us that you are its protector."

Merlin nodded. "I protect what needs no protection, I guide the quest that cannot take you anywhere, and in the end I will be there when you find the Grail, though you will see neither me nor it." Merlin looked quite pleased with this riddle and calmly emitted a puff of smoke from his mouth, as if tobacco had already been discovered.

Percival suddenly stood up. "Well, if I am the clod here, let me take my leave."

Merlin's demeanor softened slightly. "You are what you are, which seems to be good enough in God's eyes and rare enough in this hopeless world," he muttered. "Take your place, if you please." Percival, still somewhat sullen, complied with this courteous request.

"I haven't come to your fire by chance. I am here to guide

148

you to the Grail," Merlin declared. "There is a rule that cannot be disobeyed: when the pupil is ready, the master appears. What you wish to know, I can teach. My opening remarks were not rude or mystical. I only want you to clear your heads of any misguided dreams you may have about the object of your quest."

With a motion of his hand, Merlin caused the ring of fire to die down to a dull glow, so his features were barely visible by its embers. The two knights saw him mostly as a long shadow with a crown of white hair lit by the rising moon.

"The quest that brings the Grail as its prize is not a journey of the kind ignorant knights crave to mount. It is an inner journey, a quest of transformation. You both have heard tell of this thing called alchemy?" Percival and Galahad nodded, dim figures outlined by the deeper darkness. "Alchemy is the art of transformation," Merlin continued, "and when its seven steps are achieved, then and only then will you be able to summon the Grail."

"Seven steps?" Percival asked. "Then the Grail is made of gold after all, for I know that alchemists—"

"Cobwebs and rubbish. You know little or nothing about this art, yet you have practiced it every day since you were born," replied Merlin. "Every baby is born an alchemist, then loses the art, only to gain it again." It dawned on Percival that the wizard would resort to riddles if he persisted in doubting him; therefore, the knight wisely sat back and listened.

"The greatest waste in existence," Merlin said, "is the waste of spirit. Each of you mortals came into the world to seek the Grail. No one is born more privileged than any other; a wizard sees that everyone is created to reach freedom and fulfillment."

"Am I not already free?" Percival asked.

"In the simplest sense, yes, since you are not held captive, but I mean freedom in a deeper sense: the ability to do anything you want whenever you want," replied Merlin. "And there are even deeper levels. As you must admit, you are held captive all the time by the past—your memories create the conditioning that literally runs your life. If you were free from the past, you could step into infinite possibilities, breaking the barrier of the known at every moment. The Grail is just a visible promise that such perfection exists. Do you understand?"

Now that he had warmed to his subject, the wizard didn't wait for their assent. "I have said that there are seven steps of alchemy on the way to freedom and fulfillment. The first step begins at birth, the next few follow in childhood, and the rest are left to you. You are always taken care of in the divine plan, but as you grow up your own will and desire are allowed to increase. As a baby you were pure enough to seize the Grail but too ignorant to know of its existence. As an adult you know the goal, but you have already closed the way to find it. The introduction of free will is what caused you to lose the Grail, yet it is also the means by which you will recapture it in the end."

Fearing that Percival might start objecting, Galahad quickly interjected, "Will you show us the seven steps?" Merlin let a faint, knowing smile cross his lips before he nodded his assent.

STEP 1—INNOCENCE

"You were born in a state of innocence. Of all the ingredients used by the alchemist, this is the most important. A newborn baby does not question its existence; it lives in self-acceptance, trust, and love. The nagging voice of doubt is not yet heard.

"When you look in a baby's eyes, you see very little individuality. The question Who am I? is meaningless to an infant. Instead what shines through is awareness itself, the source of all wisdom. A baby comes into this world from the very source of life, and it detaches from that source gradually. For a while a baby remains bathed in the timeless. It has no concept of past or future, only an unfolding present. This is what it means to live in eternity, for what is the eternal but the present moment ever renewing itself? The very promise of the Grail—immortal life— is already being enjoyed by a baby, for living in the timeless is the secret to immortality."

"If that's true," Galahad said gravely, "then why aren't we all immortal from birth?"

"Seeds and tendencies," replied Merlin. "Every baby has a tendency to move from the timeless world to the world of hours and days and years, from the silence of the inner world to the activity of the outer world, from self-absorption to absorption in all the fascinating things around it. Watch an infant in its first few weeks of life. You can see its attention become drawn to this astonishing new world it finds itself in. And so the alchemy begins, the constant transformation that will underlie every breath taken for all the years to come.

"A baby isn't an angel—its purity has a short life span. Inside a baby feels the first twinges of anger and fear, distrust and doubt. As a baby leaves its state of innocence, it emerges into a harsher world of bumps and bruises. Desires spring up that are not immediately fulfilled; pain is experienced for the first time.

"You mortals call this the fall from grace, but you are wrong. Grace operates at every step of human existence, though your limited perception may prevent you from seeing it."

"Why is any of this sad tale akin to alchemy?" Percival asked, still feeling skeptical.

"Because there is a hidden magic at work," Merlin said. "As the baby grows its original innocence isn't really lost. What happens is more mysterious than that. Innocence remains intact in a state of purity and wholeness that you simply forget. You are living in fragments now. To you, the world is limited; your sense of self is bound up in the individual experiences and memories you've accumulated.

"By forgetting wholeness you seemed to lose who you were, yet that is an illusion. You don't feel or act like a newborn, but its essence remains. In actual fact, wholeness cannot be fragmented; truth cannot be harmed by untruth. Your loss of innocence was a real event that at the same time has no reality at all. The forces of alchemy are at work beyond what you can see, hear, or touch."

151

"How can I know that this innocence is really there?" asked Galahad.

"If you wish to contact the innocence within you, look for the characteristics of the infant: alertness, curiosity, a sense of wonder, security that you are wanted on this earth, a feeling of living in the perfect peace of the timeless. All babies feel these things."

STEP 2—BIRTH OF EGO

"The next step," Merlin continued, "announces the arrival on the scene of ego, the sense of 'I.' To have 'I,' you must also have 'you' or 'it.' The birth of ego is the birth of duality. It marks the beginning of opposites and thus the beginning of opposition. Every new step in alchemy overturns the one that came before, turning your old world upside down, but this revolution is perhaps the most shocking. You're no longer a god!

"Imagine a being who feels omnipotent in his world. Everywhere he looks all that greets his eye is a mirror of himself. Suddenly people and things start to be seen as separate creations. None of you remembers this shattering event because it occurred early in infancy. Yet it was a momentous change, amounting to a new birth. You were happy as a god, now you are born into mortality."

"It was a birth into pain too," said Percival. "Was this step absolutely necessary?"

"Oh yes. Seeds and tendencies, I told you. As a baby's curiosity pulls its attention outside itself, what does it see? First the face of its mother. In nature's plan a baby will automatically respond to its mother as a source of love and nurturing. But it is a source *outside the baby itself.* There's the catch, for however perfect motherly love will be, it is not self-love, and for many years you will sigh over the loss of perfect love, only to realize that you are nostalgic for your own self before anyone else arrived on the scene.

"At first there was no separation. When the baby touched the mother's breast or its crib or a wall, all these things seemed to be part of one flowing sensation without divisions. Soon, however, every baby comes to realize that there is something other than itself—the outside world. The ego says, 'This is me, that is not me.' Then gradually certain things become identified with 'me'—my mommy, my toys, my hunger, my pain, my bed. As soon as preferences arise, there is a whole world that isn't me—not my mommy, not my toys, and so forth."

"I cannot remember this birth, as you call it," Percival said. "But if what you say is correct, then it must be here that the Grail quest began. Where else would it begin but in separation?"

"Yes, as long as you sensed yourself as divine, there was no need for a quest to regain God's blessing," Merlin agreed. "In separation you began to look for yourself in objects and events. You lost the ability to see yourself as the true source of all that is. For the baby was not wrong to see itself as the source of life. As you began to explore the outer world and its objects became fascinating, you tied your happiness to them. This is called object referral, which came to replace the baby's self-referral."

"And this step was not lost either as the child continued to move on?" said Galahad.

"Nothing is ever lost. The birth of ego gave rise to aspects you can still sense in yourself: fear of abandonment, the need for approval, possessiveness, separation anxiety, self-concern, self-pity. You became addicted to the world, as you remain, because you were no longer fulfilled in that simple way a baby is. But do not despair, because beneath these changes a deeper force was at work."

STEP 3—BIRTH OF THE ACHIEVER

"Once you have ego," Merlin went on, "you have a world 'out there,' and a new tendency emerges, the urge to go out into the world and achieve. The first signs of this change are primitive.

153

The baby wants to grab things and hold them; it wants to explore on its own, always making sure that mother is nearby. Soon it wants to walk and begins to protest if its mother won't let it. This desire to escape and roam is timid at first. But over time the same baby that yearned to be held and protected wails to be let go. This is a healthy instinct, for the ego knows that the unknown is the source of fear. If the baby did not go out to conquer the world, it would grow to fear it more and more.

"We are now moving further away from the sense of peace, unity, and trust that you were born with. The ego starts to dominate over the spirit. When the baby reaches inside to feel what's there, it doesn't find pure awareness anymore; instead it finds a whirl of memory. Experiences become personal, never again to be fully shared."

"Another sad tale," Percival mourned.

"If it stopped here, yes," said Merlin. "But the birth of the achiever gave you confidence and a sense of uniqueness. This world of objects and events is about one thing—becoming individual. Ego is needed for that, at least on the path you mortals have chosen."

"Not everyone is an achiever. Is this a necessary step?" asked Galahad.

"Not everyone prizes success above everything else or identifies with money, work, and status," Merlin said. "But the urge of the achiever is simpler, more basic than that. It is the mark of the ego in action, proving to itself that separation is endurable. Indeed, the birth of the achiever makes this a joyous world full of things to do and learn. In some people the achiever will last a very long time. The thirst for fame and fortune will overwhelm the true purpose of the quest. But God permits complete free will, and if a person decides that the world 'out there' is more important than himself, a craving for fame and fortune must follow.

"The ego, as a wizard sees it, offers no possibility of fulfillment at all. It is controlling and loveless. 'Listen to me,' it says, 'and grab all you can for yourself. This way lies happiness.' All of you mortals follow that advice for a while. Nor is there any harm in it from God's point of view, because His trust in free will turns out to be the wisest course.

"I hardly need tell you that this third step remains with you, because as long as ego is present, the achiever will be present. The achiever never satisfies its appetites. After all, there is no limit to the experiences that you can amass; the world is infinite in its diversity. But as the ego grows, it smothers the spirit with layers of stuff—wealth, power, self-image—until a small voice begins to wonder, 'Where is love? Where is being?' The fourth step, yet another birth, is at hand."

STEP 4—BIRTH OF THE GIVER

"In time the ego hits upon a new notion," Merlin added, "that happiness lies not just in taking but also in giving. This is a momentous discovery, for it rids the ego of many kinds of fear. There is the fear of isolation, which total selfishness must lead to. There is the fear of loss, which arises because you can't hold on to everything forever. There is the fear of enemies, those who want to take from you.

"By becoming a giver, the ego doesn't have to live with these fears, at least not as much as before. A nagging problem has been solved. But there is something deeper at work too. Giving connects two people, the giver and the receiver. This connection gives birth to a new sense of belonging, not the passive belonging of the baby who automatically belongs to the mother but the active belonging of someone who has learned to create happiness.

"Giving is creative. It also turns the ego's perspective completely around. Before the giver is born, guarding against loss was all-important. This meant loss of money and possessions but also loss of self-image, loss of importance. Now the person freely parts with something, yet it doesn't *feel* like a loss. Instead the ego

155

feels pleasure. How amazing, for the pleasure of taking was never like this."

Galahad looked reflective. "Love has entered the heart. That's the difference."

"Yes," Merlin said. "As long as the ego pursues self-interest, it doesn't feel love. It may feel intense pleasure or self-satisfaction or attachment. These feelings are sometimes called love, but in its nature love is selfless, and it takes a selfless act to call love forth. Giving isn't limited to giving money or things to someone else. There is also service, the giving of oneself, and devotion, the giving of love in pure form.

"For all these reasons the birth of the giver feels new and liberating. Even though the ego still dominates, it has begun to look outside itself. Most people learn the pleasure of giving as small children; most parents teach their children to share with other children. Yet the true birth of the giver may not come until much later. As long as you are giving because you were told to, or because you think it is the right thing to do, you will not feel the deep pleasure of giving. Giving must be spontaneous, born of the sense 'This is what I want to do,' not 'This is what I'd better do.'"

"When one starts to give, is this a sign that the ego is dying?" asked Percival.

Merlin frowned. "In alchemy there is no death. Nothing has to perish in order to reach the Grail. This old notion of ego death assumes that there are things about you that God judges against."

"But you've just said that the ego is controlling and loveless," Percival objected. "Is that part of God's plan for us?"

"God's plan is for you to find yourself," Merlin said. "You are not destined just to reach a fixed goal. If you want to explore what it is like to be selfish or ignorant or murderous or totally without faith, God permits all these experiences. Why shouldn't He? Because you are not judged, none of your actions is good or bad in God's eyes."

"But that's shocking," said Galahad. "You're saying that a murderer and a saint are equal?"

"They are equal if the sinner and the saint are just masks you put on," Merlin replied. "The saint in this life may be the sinner in another life, and the sinner today may be learning to become a saint tomorrow. All these roles are illusions in God's eyes. I am not saying you must force this perspective on yourself. You asked me for guidance, however, and I must show you what lies ahead on the path."

STEP 5—BIRTH OF THE SEEKER

"For a long time the ego has had everything its way," Merlin continued. "The question What is good for me? has dominated all considerations; the limited individual viewpoint has been the only one that seemed real. This is only natural. As I said, this relative world has a purpose, to teach you to become an individual. But individuality eventually begins to open up and broaden its horizons. You might predict that given free will, humans would only indulge in more and more selfishness. If the loveless, controlling ego had the last word, perhaps this would be your fate, but alchemy works invisibly, in unseen passageways of the soul.

"In time the giver takes the next step, to the seeker. In this phase one's old, familiar ego concerns are set aside. The sense of 'I' is allowed to expand. Now the person becomes eager for spiritual experiences, sensing a source of love and fulfillment that even the most intense love of another person cannot deliver. Again this about-face comes as a shock. At his best the giver is a philanthropist. He started out by giving only to family and friends, then to charities or community, but in the end the spirit of giving can't be satisfied until all humans benefit.

"But can you really give of yourself to everyone else in the world? This question brings you to the limit of individuality; it is the question only a saint can answer. So it is natural that the stage of giving raises questions it cannot answer, thus preparing the way for a new birth. The giver who wanted to embrace the world now finds that the world is no longer a source of fulfillment. Things that once brought pleasure begin to seem flat; in particular the ego's need for approval and self-importance no longer works to bring satisfaction. A thirst arises to see the face of God, to live in the light, to explore the silence of pure awareness: the seeker's impulse can take many forms.

"Yet all seekers share a feeling that the material world does not seem to be the place where their desires can be fulfilled. Why is this? Isn't God everywhere, isn't spirit in the tiniest grain of sand? Yes and no. God may be everywhere, but that does you no good if you cannot see where He is. The seeker seeks in order to see."

"I think *this* is the stage when the Grail quest begins," said Galahad.

"For some mortals, indeed, this is when the Grail becomes a symbol for a deep inner need," Merlin replied, "but every stage has been a quest, even the fall from innocence. You mortals are obsessed with splitting up reality into good and bad, saint and sinner, godly and ungodly, when in fact life is a divine flow. A single impulse, the impulse to possess complete knowledge and complete fulfillment, is what drives all of life forward.

"Yet you are right in a sense. With the birth of the seeker, we can for the first time put a name to a desire that has remained nameless up to now. Whether the name is God, the Grail, divine Being, or spirit doesn't matter. They all point toward a new, deep-felt need to escape the boundaries imposed by time and space. Your essence is boundless. You were born to a universal life. The world seems to be limited by time and space, but that is only an appearance."

"Why do we have to be fooled by appearances?" asked Percival.

"The universe isn't hiding anything from you," Merlin replied. "You aren't being tricked. The appearance of limitation

158

arises because this world is a school, or training ground. And the basic rule here is that however you see yourself, so you will see the world. If you see yourself as lacking or unworthy, that judgment alone will keep God from you. You may say that you want God, but you want to keep up these judgments against yourself at the same time."

"So God stays away," Galahad said mournfully. "And the quest of the Grail is neverending."

Merlin gave him a sympathetic look. "Spirit could not stay away from you even if it wanted to, because everything is spirit. There are no secret places where it does not live. For His part, God sees nothing wrong with you.

"Let me speak to you more about the seeker, for this is the stage of alchemy that draws the wizard to you, and it is also the stage for which mortals find themselves least prepared. Since you were a baby you have desired more and more. The seeker is simply one whose desires have expanded to the point that nothing will satisfy them short of meeting God face-to-face. This is not a 'higher' desire than wanting toys or money or fame or love. Toys, money, fame, and love *were* the face of God when they were the most important things to you. Anything that you believe will bring you final peace and fulfillment is your version of God. As you grow from one phase to the next, however, you get closer to the real goal; your image of God becomes truer, nearer to His nature as pure spirit. Yet every step is divine."

"Are you saying that someone who wants to steal or commit murder is following a divine impulse? After all, these are desires too," said Percival.

"Love is universal, and therefore it takes no sides," replied Merlin. "The ego may not like this fact. It may say, 'I deserve God's love but that person over there doesn't.' This is not God's perspective. The thief inflicts loss of property; the murderer inflicts loss of life. As long as these losses are real to you, then of course you will condemn the person who causes them. But will not time itself also steal your property and life in the end? Is time a criminal too?

There is a perspective that looks upon sin as illusion. Nothing you call sin can blemish God's love by the least iota."

"Do seekers automatically get the visions and experiences they desire?" asked Galahad.

"Everyone gets the version of the divine that he or she conceives in the mind. Some see God in visions, some in a flower. There are many kinds of seekers. Some require acts of miraculous intervention and redemption, others follow an invisible force that speaks in the most mundane occurrences. The seeker is simply motivated by a thirst for higher reality. This doesn't mean that the earlier stage of giving disappears. But now the giving is done without selfish motivation, now it comes out of compassion.

"For the first time the ego's claim to be all-knowing and all-powerful is questioned. The birth of the seeker therefore can be extremely turbulent. Imagine yourself as a carriage pulled down the road by a team of horses. For the longest time there is no driver, and the horses have come to believe that they own the carriage. Then one day a soft voice from inside the carriage whispers, 'Stop.' At first the horses don't hear the voice, but it repeats, 'Stop.' Unable to believe their ears, the horses race even more wildly ahead, just to prove that they have no master. The inner voice doesn't use force; it doesn't protest. It only continues to repeat, 'Stop.'

"That is what happens inside you. The carriage is your total self, the horses are the ego, the voice inside the carriage is spirit. When spirit announces itself on the scene, the ego at first doesn't listen, because it is certain that its power is absolute. But spirit doesn't use the kind of power that ego is accustomed to. Ego is used to rejecting things; it is used to judging and separating and taking what it thinks belongs to it. Spirit is simply the quiet voice of Being, asserting what is. With the birth of the seeker, this is the voice you start to hear, but you must be prepared for a violent reaction from the ego, which after all is not going to surrender its power without a struggle."

"How does this struggle ever come to an end if spirit doesn't have any power?" asked Percival.

"I said that spirit doesn't use power as the ego knows it. In time you will learn that spirit is nothing but power, power of infinite scope. It is an organizing power that keeps every atom in the universe in perfect balance. Compared with it, the ego's power is absurdly limited and trivial. However, this realization will dawn only after you have surrendered the ego's need to control, predict, and defend. Its power is limited to these three things. If your ego could surrender all at once, there wouldn't be any need for later steps of growth; the birth of the seeker would be enough.

"This isn't the case, however. The voice of spirit announces that there is a higher reality. Ascending to that reality is another matter."

"I would think seekers must be rare, given how hard the struggle is," said Galahad. "Many must fail and lose hope. Is that why so few are born to attain the Grail?"

"Everyone is born to attain the Grail," Merlin reminded him. "The reason that seekers seem to be rare is mostly a matter of social appearances. Seeking is a completely inward experience. You cannot tell from outer signs who is seeking and who isn't. Society holds out no special distinctions or rewards for the seeker, who may completely retreat into isolation, leaving society behind, or who may continue to live a life of high position."

"How will a person know that he is a seeker?" asked Percival.

"The inward marks of the seeker are these: giving becomes motivated by selfless love and compassion, wanting nothing in return, not even gratitude; intuition becomes a trustworthy guide to action, replacing strict rationality; one catches glimpses of an unseen world as the higher reality; intimations of God and immortality appear. These signs will be accompanied by growing enjoyment of solitude, by self-reliance in place of social approval, by stirrings of Being, and by a willingness to trust. Addictive patterns will start to disappear. Meditation and prayer

161

become parts of daily life. Yet as all these spiritual manifestations pull you away from the material world, you will find, paradoxically, a deeper connection to nature, more comfort in your body, and easier acceptance of other people. This is because spirit is not the opposite of matter. Spirit is everything, and its appearance in your life will make all things better, even things that appear to be opposites."

STEP 6—BIRTH OF THE SEER

"I told you," Merlin went on, "that the seeker's motivation was to be able to see, and soon this emerges. The sixth step, the birth of the seer, is just below the surface of any seeker. By itself seeking carries no fulfillment; it would be a dry and frustrating life if you were only to seek without finding. Fortunately, in the divine plan all questions bring their answers at the same time, all goals turn out to be found at the source. Once you truly ask Where is God? you will see a response.

"I don't want to delude you here. The birth of the seer is just as revolutionary as any of the earlier steps. It spells the end of the ego, the end of all outward identification. Imagine that your life is a moving picture projected upon a white screen. As long as you are dominated by ego, you focus on the moving images and take them to be real. When the seeker arrives on the scene, you begin to sense their unreality. But with the birth of the seer, you turn and face the light. Now self-image is seen for what it is, a flimsy projection made real by the ego's desperate need to place importance on the time-bound mind and body.

"The seer sees through this motivation and no longer buys into it. Instead of seeing yourself as flesh and bones that house a spirit—a ghost inside a machine—you realize that everything is spirit. The body is spirit coalesced into a form that the senses can feel, see, and smell; the mind is spirit in a form that can be heard and understood. Spirit itself, in pure form, is neither of these and can be perceived only by refined intuition. You have heard the phrase 'Those who know It speak of It not; those who speak of It know It not.' Such is the mystery of spirit."

"But aren't you speaking of It right now?" asked Galahad, looking confused.

"Not in the way you may think. When I speak of a rock, you can see and touch it. When I speak of spirit, I am pointing toward an invisible world. Arrows of light fly to us from that world to ignite our souls, but we cannot send arrows of thought back."

"That sounds very mysterious," muttered Percival.

"A rose would be mysterious if you could only think about it and never experience one. Spirit is a direct experience, but it transcends this world. It is pure silence teeming with infinite potential. When you gain knowledge of anything else, you gain knowledge of some thing; when you gain knowledge of spirit, you become knowingness itself. All questions cease because you find yourself in the womb of reality, where everything simply *is*. When the eye of the seer falls on something, it is simply accepted for what it is, not judged. There is no ego need to take or possess or destroy. In the absence of fear, no such motivations arise, for needing to possess is born of lack. When you have no lack to fill, then just being here in this world in your body is the highest spiritual goal you could possibly attain."

Percival and Galahad were much struck by this part of Merlin's discourse. They had followed the early steps with attention, but the ego, the achiever, and the giver were all familiar already. When the wizard spoke of the seeker, the two knights saw themselves as they were at that moment. The seer, however, filled them with awe, as if they were explorers arriving on a mountaintop and surveying a vast new horizon long hoped for but not yet experienced.

"I long to be this seer you speak of," Galahad said fervently.

Merlin nodded. "Which means you are ready. To a wizard there are only three kinds of people: those who have not yet experienced pure Being, those who have tasted it, and those who have fully explored it. You have tasted and now want to explore. For you

163

this world will begin to disappear as a solid thing and recede into the overwhelming light of Being. In a faraway land called India they say that ordinary life becomes pale before God, like a candle that seemed bright in a dark room but turns invisible when put out into the noonday sun." He turned to Percival. "And I include you in this stage too, however you imagine I judged you."

Percival turned scarlet, then stammered, "What will this new life be like?"

"As always, it will feel like a new birth. The seer differs from the seeker in no longer having to pick and choose. The seeker is still involved in an illusion as he goes around saying, 'This is where God is, this is where God isn't.' The seer, on the other hand, sees God in life itself. The long inner war is over at last, and rest comes to the warrior. In place of struggle, you experience all your desires naturally and effortlessly coming true. There are no outward signs to mark who are the seers among us, but inwardly they feel open and content, they allow others to be who they will be, which is the highest form of love, they put up no obstruction to other people and events, and they have surrendered any small sense of 'I.' "

STEP 7—SPIRIT

"It's hard to imagine that there could be any higher stage of life," Galahad said after a moment, deeply moved by Merlin's description of the seer.

"Be careful with that word *higher*," cautioned Merlin. "It's the ego that must have high and low. The goal of your life is freedom and fulfillment. Fulfillment isn't achieved until you know God as completely as He knows Himself. You mortals are always yearning for miracles, and I tell you that the greatest miracle is yourselves, for God has given you this unique ability to identify with His nature. A perfect rose does not sense that it is a rose; a fulfilled human knows what it means to be divine."

"Can this state be described?" asked Percival.

"It is the seventh and final step of alchemy, pure spirit. When it dawns the seer finds that what seems to be total joy and fulfillment can still expand. You see, arriving in the presence of God is not the end of your quest but the beginning. You began in innocence, and so shall you end. But this time the innocence is different, because you have gained complete knowledge, whereas a baby has only feeling.

"When you are able to see yourself as spirit, your identification with this body and this mind will cease. At the same time the concept of birth and death will cease. You will be a cell in the body of the universe, and this cosmic body will be as intimate to you as your own body is to you now. That is the closest I can come to how a wizard feels, for *wizard* is just another word for the seventh stage.

"Understand this: birth for a wizard is merely the idea that 'I have this body,' and death is merely the idea that 'I no longer have this body.' Since wizards are not subject to the illusion of birth, any body they take on is seen as a pattern of energy, any mind as a pattern of information. These patterns forever change; they come and go. But the wizard himself is beyond change. Mind and body are like rooms one might choose to live in, but not all the time.

"No amount of thinking or feeling can approximate this state or bring it to you. Spirit is born of pure silence. Your mind's internal dialogue must end and never begin again, because what gave rise to the inner dialogue—fragmentation of the self—is no longer present. Your self will be unified, and like the baby that was your beginning, you will feel no doubt, shame, or guilt. The ego's need for duality resulted in a world of good and bad, right and wrong, light and shadow. Now you will see that these opposites are fused. Such is God's perspective, for everywhere He looks, all He sees is Himself.

"If you feel that this goal is too lofty or too far off, here is a secret. Although you seem to pass through the seven steps of alchemy, each one was present from the beginning. In innocence

165

was the totality of God, as it is in ego or achieving or giving or seeking. All that truly changed was your focus of attention. In your being is every aspect of the universe, as complete and eternal as the universe itself. But still the birth into spirit is a tremendous event. As unity ripens you will become more and more familiar with the divine, until finally you will experience God as an infinite being moving at infinite speed through infinite dimensions. When that awesome experience dawns, it will seem as natural and simple as sitting here under the stars, yet each dancing star will be yourself."

As often happens when wizards speak, the two knights felt themselves transported into the very state he was describing. Galahad looked up at the night sky and suddenly felt as if he could touch the stars. A sense of truly belonging in the world suffused his heart. "We are home," Percival whispered to himself.

"Do not be overawed," Merlin murmured. "These feelings have such intensity because they are new to you. In truth this is your natural state. To be unified with the cosmos, to be intimate with life in all its forms, to finally come into oneness with your own Being—this is your destiny, the end of your quest."

"In the end we shall return to the beginning," Galahad murmured.

"Yes," said Merlin. "Each of you begins with love, goes through struggle, passion, and suffering, only to end in love again." Merlin's voice grew softer as the circle of light around them faded almost to nothing. "You mortals long for miracles, I say, and as privileged children of the universe, you will be denied nothing. Spirit is the state of the miraculous, which will unfold to you in three stages:

"*First,* you will experience miracles in the state called cosmic consciousness. Every material event will have a spiritual cause. Every local happening will also be taking place on the stage of the universe. Your slightest wish will cause cosmic forces to bring about its fulfillment. As wonderful as that sounds, it is not such an advanced state, for long before you reach cosmic consciousness you will be used to having your desires spontaneously come true.

"*Second,* you will perform miracles in the state called divine consciousness. This is the state of pure creativity, in which you fuse with God's power, whereby He makes worlds and all that happens in those worlds. This power comes from nothing God does—it is just His light of awareness. Like a rich, golden glow, you will see the divine awareness shining through everything your eyes behold. The world becomes illuminated from within, and there is no doubt that matter is simply spirit made manifest. In divine consciousness you will see yourself as the creator, not the created, the giver of life, not the receiver.

"*Third,* you will become the miracle, in the state known as unity consciousness. Now any distinction between creator and created has vanished. The spirit within you totally merges with the spirit in everything else. Your return to innocence is all-enveloping, because, like the baby who touches the wall or the crib and feels only himself, you will see every action as spirit pouring into spirit. You will live in complete knowingness and trust. And although you will seem to reside still in a body, it will be only a grain of Being on the shores of the infinite ocean of Being that is yourself."

The two knights had no notion of how long this exposition of Merlin's had taken. They seemed to have been lifted into a space where spheres of Being opened one after another like flower petals. And as the last opened a nearly transparent diamond could barely be seen rotating in its center. "What is it?" Galahad wanted to ask but dared not.

"*Behold the Grail,*" Merlin whispered. "The unfolding of your quest has led to a vision of the goal—the point of pure light, the diamond essence that burns within your soul." The two knights knelt on the cold ground and prayed in their hearts to be worthy of the vision. "Live in devotion to this moment," said Merlin. "I have led you here out of your innermost desire, but now you must win the true Grail, not just its vision, for yourself."

"The true Grail?" Percival murmured. "What should we look for, this same image?"

"Do not expect, do not anticipate," cautioned Merlin as the vision of the Grail began to disappear. "Man quests for symbols, and symbols change from age to age. But what I have shown you is not a symbol but the truth. The Grail is the crystal speck of Being in your own heart. It faintly reflects light from its facets, and from those faint reflections arise all the faculties of mind and body that you perceive with your senses. As reflections they are real, but far more real is this transparent diamond of pure Being."

Unexpectedly Merlin yawned, tilting his head back as if it were the most enjoyable act in the world. He stretched his arms wide and stood up. It was nearly pitch black now, all the fire having gone out, but Percival and Galahad could feel Merlin's eyes fixed upon them. He said, "One day you will look back upon this night and ask, 'Who are you, Merlin?' From beyond the reach of time I answer you thus: I am the one who has no need for miracles. I am a wizard, and for me to be here is miracle enough. What could be more miraculous than life itself?"

With the last fading of the light, the old one was gone. Percival and Galahad stood still, without a word. The spell of Merlin's speech still held them, and as it started to fade, they both trembled, regretting their return to earth. When dawn broke they began to make their way back to the castle. In the golden birth of the sun, Percival saw King Arthur standing at the window of his royal chambers; he was looking directly at them.

"Do you think we should tell him of this?" Percival asked, gesturing toward the castle.

Galahad shook his head. "I am certain that the king knows what has happened; it must have happened to him, or why else would he be so reluctant to speak of the Grail? But I tell you this, Brother Knight. I would like Arthur to understand that we are with him in this quest of Merlin's. Let us agree to call this the night of the crystal cave. The king will know what we mean."

And although they had been in no cave but out under the canopy of a spangled sky, Percival instantly agreed.

ABOUT THE AUTHOR

Deepak Chopra is the author of fifteen books and more than thirty audio- and videotape series, including the critically acclaimed public television show *Body, Mind and Soul: The Magic and the Mystery* and the forthcoming public television special based on this book. His works have been translated into twenty-five languages.

For information on other books, and audio and videotapes by
Deepak Chopra, please contact:

Quantum Publications Inc.
PO Box 1008
Sudbury, MA 01776
1–800–858–1808

The Way of the Wizard is also available on videocassette.
For information contact:

Mystic Fire Video
PO Box 422
New York, NY 10012
1–800–292–9001